Raising an
Active Reader

Raising an Active Reader

The Case for Reading Aloud to Engage Elementary School Youngsters

Samantha Cleaver

ROWMAN & LITTLEFIELD
Lanham • Boulder • New York • London

Published by Rowman & Littlefield
An imprint of The Rowman & Littlefield Publishing Group, Inc.
4501 Forbes Boulevard, Suite 200, Lanham, Maryland 20706
www.rowman.com

6 Tinworth Street, London SE11 5AL, United Kingdom

British Library Cataloguing in Publication Information Available

Library of Congress Cataloging-in-Publication Data Available

ISBN 9781475849288 (cloth: alk. paper)
ISBN 9781475849295 (electronic)

∞™ The paper used in this publication meets the minimum requirements of American National Standard for Information Sciences—Permanence of Paper for Printed Library Materials, ANSI/NISO Z39.48-1992.

For Reuben and my three Active Readers,
Saha, Neina, and Katali.

Contents

Acknowledgments

This book would not have been possible without help and encouragement from my family or without the help of the parents who gave their own perspectives on Active Reading: Erin, Kate, Monica, Angie, Lindsay, and Heather. The idea of Active Reading would not be possible without Read Charlotte and the original research and work on *Read with Me: Engaging Your Young Child in Active Reading*. Finally, I am indebted to the people who filled my life with books growing up, my parents and teachers.

Introduction

One spring afternoon, I opened a new picture book, *Ida, Always* by Caron Levis, to read with my five-year-old. The story is about two polar bears, Gus and Ida, who live together at the Central Park Zoo. The two bears enjoy playing together, but then Ida gets sick and eventually dies. Gus, sad and angry, continues on alone, although he sees memories of Ida everywhere.

At the time I read this book, my daughter, like many children, was curious about death. The text is straightforward about Ida's illness and passing, so we talked about what was happening and how Gus felt about it. My daughter asked questions: What happened to Ida? How did she die? Where did she go? Long after we read the story, my daughter returned to the story with more questions: Did the zoo get another polar bear? Will I ever get sick and die, like Ida?

Reading *Ida, Always* and processing the experience of death, even through the story of two polar bears, helped my daughter better conceptualize something she was curious about. It also helped her conceptualize a topic that is difficult to understand. Talking about the story also helped reinforce the idea that books can help her understand and connect to big ideas.

This understanding, and the conversation that we had about *Ida, Always*, is the power of a picture book. Through this simple story about two polar bears, we had discussions about death. She got to see how this topic played out in one relationship. Then she took the emotions and situation on in her own way. This is the power of Active Reading, which takes the act of reading *to* kids and transforms it into reading *with* kids, letting them lead and direct the discussion about a story to satisfy their curiosity and interests, and building the foundation for future reading success.

ACTIVE READING: PREPARING YOUR CHILD
FOR READING SUCCESS

You may have heard that third grade is an important benchmark year when it comes to reading.[1] When children are able to read on grade level—in third grade, that's a child who can pick up, read, and enjoy *Charlotte's Web* by E. B. White—they're better prepared for the demands of school as they move into upper elementary school. When children start fourth grade, they're expected to read on their own and learn information from books in ways that they're not in the younger grades.

Starting in fourth grade, children will be given a text, an article, or novel, and will be expected to read it before they use the information. They may, for example, read an article about volcanoes and then come to a small group to share what they learned. Or they may read a chapter of a novel and meet with a small group to discuss. Of course, children will have support as they learn to use text, but the better prepared they are to make the transition from "learning to read" to "reading to learn" in mid-elementary school, the better (more on this in Chapter 2).

Early reading experiences make the difference for kids as they prepare to be successful readers. As children experience Active Reading, as they learn to understand and answer questions, build their vocabulary, and learn new information that adds to what they already know, they are creating the foundation of knowledge and skills that they will use to read on their own, in third grade and beyond. For example, a child who is interested in sharks and learns facts about sharks through reading aloud with their parents will be well prepared to read about sharks on their own as they learn how to sound out words from *dorsal fin* to *nocturnal* to learn more about sharks on their own.

WHAT IS ACTIVE READING?

In short, Active Reading is a way to read *with*, rather than *to*, children. The goal of Active Reading is not just to read a book, telling them the story or information, but to engage them in conversation and thinking about the story or topic. When you are using the Active Reading techniques with your child (the ABCs of Active Reading), you'll hear from your child—their ideas, their questions, their connections—more often than you would when you are reading *to* them. In Active Reading, it's your child who is "active." It's not about you acting out the story—adding voices to characters or exaggerating the suspense in a scene—although those can be a part of reading aloud. Instead, the goal is that your child is actively engaging with and thinking about what you're reading together.

Active Reading was created from research on dialogic reading, a method of reading with young children (ages two to five) that focuses on having young children engage in conversation through picture book reading.[2] Active Reading for young children is covered in the book *Read with Me: Engaging Your Child in Active Reading* (2018) that I cowrote with Munro Richardson, executive director of Read Charlotte, a nonprofit in Charlotte, North Carolina. In our work, we distilled the techniques of dialogic reading into the ABCs of Active Reading: Ask questions, Build vocabulary, and Connect to the child's world. We also crystalized the goal of reading with your child, to have a conversation about the story. Think of it as a one-on-one book club with your child.

Now Active Reading, specifically for children age two to five, is being shared throughout Charlotte and Mecklenburg County, North Carolina, as part of the local initiative to boost reading proficiency across the county. Thinking about children age five through nine (roughly kindergarten through third grade), we know that Active Reading techniques can be extended to older children, and that they benefit older children in unique ways, which is how this book came about. In the research, dialogic reading strategies, often called *shared reading* or *interactive shared reading*, have been expanded to reach the needs of children in elementary school who are learning to read on their own.

As children grow as readers, how they engage with books changes. Yes, they'll be reading on their own. Their ability to think through and analyze stories will develop. They'll have their own opinions about characters, stories, authors, and topics. And, they'll want to venture out on their own—exploring stories and topics that they share with friends rather than with you. But the need to engage children in the ABCs of Active Reading remains through the elementary school years and even into middle and high school.

The research on reading aloud with older children (age five through eight) has gone into shaping the ABCs of Active Reading with children who are in elementary school. The goal of this book is to extend and expand Active Reading to older children. Through reading and using the tools in this book, you will meet the needs of your budding reader, teach them important skills they can use when they read on their own, and connect with your child using more complex and interesting texts.

Raising a reader happens across years of reading sessions, from when your child fits neatly in your lap through read-alouds at the kitchen table when they are in school and possibly when you read together as a family. For such an important aspect of how you involve your children and family in reading, this book complements and extends books like *The Read-Aloud Handbook* by Jim Trelease[3] and *The Read Aloud Family* by Sarah Mackenzie.[4] Both those books are about why and how to build a love of reading through reading aloud. *Raising an Active Reader* tackles the how of reading aloud—what can you do while reading aloud with your children that will ensure they take the benefits of reading into their own reading lives.

That said, Active Reading and the ABCs can feel focused on academics. It may feel like you're trying to pack as much into each read-aloud session as you can, even at the cost of instilling a love of reading or having reading together be all about togetherness. However, it's important to note, too, that Active Reading should always be fun. It should always be an enjoyable experience to share a book with your child. The "cuddle factor" should always be there. If Active Reading is ever not fun, or ever starts to feel like homework or a "have to," stop! If Active Reading becomes boring, you have my permission to put down the book and connect with your child another way.

You can use the Active Reading strategies with any book or reading material (magazines, graphic novels), and with many experiences that your child will find fun. The point is to engage in conversation about what you're looking at or thinking about.

THE CASE FOR READ-ALOUD WHEN KIDS CAN READ ON THEIR OWN

We like reading with our kids, and they like reading with us. According to the 2016 Scholastic *Kids and Family Reading Report*, more than 80 percent of parents of kids ages six to eleven liked reading to their kids. Kids (87 percent) liked reading with their parents as well. Furthermore, reading aloud was a fun thing to do; 66 percent of kids and 67 percent of parents said that reading aloud was "fun." It was a special time of the day according to 72 percent of kids and 77 percent of parents. But, despite enjoying reading together, as kids got older, parents read aloud with them less and less.

On the whole, we do read aloud with younger children. A majority (62 percent) of parents read with kids age three to five regularly (five to seven days a week). But by the time the kids were in elementary school (age six to eight), only 38 percent of kids were read to regularly. By the time they were in later elementary school (age nine to eleven), that dropped to 17 percent.[5]

There are many potential reasons for this drop in reading aloud. Kids start reading on their own and parents may not see a need to continue reading to them. The day gets busy with school and work and there is no time to read aloud together. Or parents fall out of the habit of reading aloud. Whatever the reason, I'll make the case that reading aloud with your child as they get older can be a beloved part of the day that benefits you and your child. It's something you should put back into your family schedule, even if it's just fifteen minutes during bedtime.

As routines go, reading together is one that can get you the most "bang for your buck" in terms of togetherness, closeness, and academic benefits that spill over into the rest of your child's world. Here are just a few of the results of reading aloud with your elementary school–aged child: they experience books they can't read on their own, you can read about complex topics, you're building empathy, and you're keeping books front and center in their lives.

Author and educator Jim Trelease[6] advocates for reading aloud because of its immediate and long-term benefits. Your child's ability to read difficult text won't catch up with how well they can understand what's read or said to them until eighth grade. So, through read-aloud, you can expose your child to stories they're not ready to read yet, but are ready to listen to. For example, you can read a book with a higher reading level, like classic fantasy stories like *The Hobbit* by J. R. R. Tolkien, historical novels like *Bud, Not Buddy* by Christopher Paul Curtis, or modern classics like *Esperanza Rising* by Pam Munoz Ryan, with your child long before they can tackle the book on their own. (More about the benefits of reading complex texts in Chapters 4–8.)

As your child grows, they'll be curious about big topics (recall how my daughter was able to think through the idea of death after reading *Ida, Always*). Those topics and conversations only get more serious. Literature is one way to help them make sense of and understand topics that relate to and interest them. Stories, from picture books about the theme of friendship and bullying, to novels that tackle the same topic in a different context, set the stage for conversations that teach your child what they'll experience and how to deal with it. Suffice it to say, your child will probably remember the story you read about bullying and the conversation you had about it more than your lecture on the same topic. (More on connecting with fiction in Chapter 6.)

More so than when you read aloud to your preschooler, reading aloud with elementary schoolers can build important social-emotional skills, like empathy. In general, levels of empathy, the ability to understand and relate to others' feelings, are decreasing.[7] This is a concern because kids today also need to understand and relate to lots of different issues that they may never experience firsthand in order to solve them. One solution to a lack of empathy is reading, and meeting many different characters and experiencing lots of different situations in books. Reading about the experience of a girl's life under Taliban rule in *The Breadwinner* series by Deborah Ellis, the experience of trying to learn English and find a new life in the United States in the picture book *Tomàs and the Library Lady* by Pat Mora, or the experience of a child who feels left out in *The Invisible Boy* by Trudy Ludwig, gives kids who have not and will not have those experiences insight that they can take to understand real-life situations. (More on how Active Reading develops empathy in Chapter 6.)

Reading aloud for fifteen minutes a few times a week is a way to take small steps toward the big goal of raising children who are critical thinkers, strong readers, and who love books. Consider this: as long as we read to our children, we're keeping books in their lives. As parents, what we put in front of our kids matters. There is some wiggle room, to be sure, and as our kids grow, they can and should start making their own choices. But prioritizing reading together, even beyond elementary school, keeps books and reading front and center.

As Trelease points out, you have to sell books to get your kids to buy into reading. When you're excited about starting the next book about Anna Hibiscus (a book collection by Atinuke), or caught up in conversation about how an *A to Z Mystery* by Ron Roy will turn out, you're showing your kids that reading can be entertainment. They'll buy into books if you show them how, and Active Reading is a great way to keep "selling" books to your kids.[8]

READY TO READ WITH ME MORE

As children grow, even as they start to read on their own, reading aloud should be part of their "reading diet," or the way they experience books each day. Reading aloud has important benefits for children in early elementary school (ages five through nine, or grades K–3). This book provides information about how to support your child's reading skills through Active Reading with your elementary school–aged child by applying Active Reading research and principles—the ABCs of Active Reading—to fiction and nonfiction picture books, chapter books, and novels.

If you've already read *Read with Me: Engaging Your Young Child in Active Reading*, it may not seem necessary to read another book on Active Reading. But the ABCs change with your child. Asking questions is less about asking general, open-ended questions and more about asking questions that challenge your child to talk about their understanding of the text and then go beyond to analyze and think critically. Building vocabulary encompasses more as the words your child is learning become more complicated, and they need to understand phrases and figurative language as well. And connecting is not about connecting what they read to the world they experience. Instead, it's about building knowledge through reading and connecting what they know to new information and developing important social-emotional skills, like empathy, through making connections with what they read. All along the way, Active Reading is a way to keep your child engaged and interested in books alongside the work they are doing in school.

The goal of this book is to equip you with the knowledge and skills to engage your child in conversation about stories, novels, and nonfiction topics they are interested in, using the books they are reading as a springboard for that conversation. Along the way, you'll learn about the ABCs of Active Reading and how to ask important questions that get at comprehension and conversation (Chapter 4). You'll build your child's vocabulary, preparing them for later reading success (Chapter 5). And you'll learn how to generate connections between your child and what they read, both fiction and nonfiction (Chapters 6 and 7).

This book also includes information about how to support your child as they become a reader in their own right with an overview of how reading develops, and how to support your child—whether they are a typically developing reader (Chapter 2) or one of the many who struggle (Chapter 9). The goal with this information is to better prepare you to help your child at home and be a partner with your child's teacher at school.

The appendices provide additional information about books to read with your child (Appendix A) and more support from specific questions (Appendix B). Finally, I have drawn on the experiences of parents who have been there—reading with their kids among all the other things that parents need to do. Parenting is hard. Raising a child who loves books, in addition to keeping them fed and clothed, all while developing their independence can seem a daunting task. Active Reading should be one of the most fun and most rewarding times you carve out of each day. Let's read!

* * *

WHAT TO REMEMBER

- Active Reading is a way to read *with*, rather than *to*, children.
- In Active Reading, your child is active, and the goal is to have a conversation about what you are reading and to hear your child's thoughts and ideas.
- Active Reading was originally developed from evidence-based techniques of dialogic reading and expanded to address the needs of children in elementary school who are learning how to read on their own, and who are interested in more complex topics and stories.
- There are many reasons to keep reading aloud to your child as they grow:
  - You can read complex texts and more advanced stories with your child before they can read them on their own.

- ○ You can use books and stories as a starting point to tackle big ideas and tough topics.
  - ○ Reading aloud builds empathy in kids at a critical time in their lives and in our world.
  - ○ Reading aloud keeps books front and center as a thing that's important to you and your family, so you can keep "selling" reading to your kids.
- Active Reading should always be a fun activity; if it starts feeling like a "have-to" or homework, stop!

1

Keep Reading with Me

As a parent, I've watched my daughter grow from an infant, listening to me reading board books while she sat on my lap, to a reader in her own right, reading books like *Amelia Bedelia* by Peggy Parish and *Frog and Toad* by Arnold Lobel on her own. This transformation has taken five years, but it seems like it happened in moments. There was the first time she chose her own book for me to read. The first time she "read" a picture book on her own by reciting her own version of what was happening on the pages. The first time I read her a chapter book. The first time she read a book to me.

Thinking about your own child:

- What milestones have they achieved as a reader?
- What memories have you already created around reading?
- What do you think your child will remember about reading during their childhood?
- What favorite books have you shared?
- What books have you read so many times you can recite them by memory?
- What next reading milestone is your child on the cusp of?

Imagine a kindergartener poring over a new book, running their finger under each word they sound out. Unable to read in their head, they say each word as it comes to them. "The. Cat. Sat. On. The. Mat." Sometimes they laugh out loud. Sometimes they are silent for minutes at a time, studying the pictures. After they finish the story, they eagerly tell you about everything they've read.

As children move from preschool to kindergarten and into elementary school, Active Reading moves with them. When children are in their preschool years, Active Reading looks loud and excited with children pointing to the pages of a picture book, completing familiar refrains in the story, and talking about the words they come across.[1] With a first or second grader, it may be more subdued—reading a picture book with longer stretches of text and asking questions every page or so. And with a third or fourth grader, it may involve reading chapters of a novel, stopping after important or surprising scenes to talk about your reactions. How Active Reading looks will change with your child. As they move into reading on their own, Active Reading continues to be an important way for children to engage with picture books, chapter books that you'll read together, and eventually the books they read on their own.

Reading with your children may be an established part of your day, or something new. However reading aloud fits into your daily schedule, it is never too early or too late to start Active Reading with your child—both to share the experience and to improve their reading skills. Even if your child is able to read on their own, Active Reading can play an important role in fostering a love of reading simply by making reading a fun time for you to spend together.

This chapter provides an overview of what Active Reading is and is not in the elementary years. This includes an overview of the research that supports Active Reading (also called *shared reading* or *interactive reading*) with children who are in grades K–3. It provides a summary of the ABCs of Active Reading: Ask questions, Build vocabulary, make Connections. Finally, this chapter includes a discussion about the importance of continuing to read with children even after they can read on their own.

ACTIVE READING IN THE EARLY ELEMENTARY YEARS

In Erin Pavon's house, either Pavon or her husband reads to their three boys (twins age six and their five-year-old brother). Each boy choses a book for their parents to read. The boys interrupt with a stream of questions about the story and new words they hear in each book. Pavon enjoys the time because she knows that someday her boys won't want to be read to anymore. For now, she says, "they love it and they're interested."

In the long run, Pavon hopes all their reading together fosters a love of books and stories in her boys. "I really don't think there is anything more important than loving to read because it opens them up to so many new ideas," she says. Pavon is onto something. The research about how our kids' brains engage with books is clear: kids learn a lot from books, starting with picture books.

Elementary School–Aged Children Learn (a Lot) from Picture Books

We know that reading picture books to young children (preschoolers, age two to five) has a profound effect on their brains. A recent study examined how children's brains were activated when they listened to a story three different ways. When the children listened only (like an audiobook), the children did not get enough information for their brains to understand and they didn't make connections across different areas in their brains. When the children watched an animated version of the story (like a video), there was a lot of activity in both the listening and seeing networks in the brain, but not a lot of connection between the parts of their brains. This way of watching a story seemed to be too overwhelming and produced the lowest rate of understanding. But when the children were read a story and could see illustrations (like being read a picture book), they understood the story the best and the various networks in their brains connected with each other.[2] That's the work that your child's brain is doing when you read to them, connecting different parts of the brain as they listen and look at the same time.

As children get older, and their brains and language matures, it can be difficult to see the benefit of maintaining a read-aloud routine. Aren't picture books too babyish? Shouldn't kids be reading to themselves? (And, as a parent, isn't it nice to be out of the phase where kids need constant attention?)

Children in grades kindergarten through third still benefit from reading picture books, and the picture books that are just right for them are a step more advanced than what you may have read when they were in preschool. For example, *Last Stop on Market Street* by Matt de la Peña is the story of a little boy who takes a bus trip with his grandmother to visit a soup kitchen. In this book, children can follow along with CJ's experiences and relate to the experience of going on an errand that they aren't particularly invested in, as well as the experience of giving back through the soup kitchen. Older children are also better able to understand and talk about the topics of difference and fairness in the book in a way that younger children aren't ready for. Finally, older children can connect with the language used in the book—metaphors that describe rain and the feeling of listening to music are all too complex for preschoolers, but add to the reading experience for older children. Reading *Last Stop on Market Street* with preschoolers, you may talk about what CJ and his grandma did, but with elementary schoolers, you can talk about what happened, CJ's feelings and reactions, and what our obligation is to make the world a better place.

Another example, the traditional folktale *Strega Nona* by Tomie dePaola tells the story of Strega Nona or "Grandma Witch" in Italy who can make spaghetti with a magic pot, and what happens when she leaves her helper, Big Anthony, in charge of the pot. Big Anthony has seen Strega Nona make spaghetti and tries to replicate it on his own, but he misses a key step and the pot won't stop. The pasta overtakes the town and Strega Nona has to fix it and punish Big Anthony when she returns.

This story itself is simple enough, but older children can have discussions about the themes of trust and punishment that younger children aren't ready for. Reading this folktale and others using Active Reading, you can talk about questions like, Who should decide someone's punishment? What makes someone trustworthy? Should Strega Nona have trusted Big Anthony? All these questions are good ways to engage children in discussion about big ideas that come from picture books.

ACTIVE READING: EVIDENCE-BASED BEDTIME READING

A class of first-grade students sat in their assigned carpet spots, waiting to start the day's book: Alexander and the Terrible, Horrible, No Good, Very Bad Day *by Judith Viorst. It's the second time they've read the story of Alexander's awful day. The teacher begins by posting a vocabulary word on the board:* scrunched.

"Scrunched means smashed," the teacher says. "What is scrunched in the story?"

The first graders wave their hands in the air.

"Alexander was scrunched in the backseat of the car," one replies.

"That's right. Now, today we're going to think about how Alexander feels during the story."

In classrooms, Active Reading incorporates asking and answering questions, clear teaching of new words, and helping children connect what they already know to better understand new information they find in books. The goal is to get students talking about what they read, with the teacher or with each other.

Researchers have studied Active Reading, like the previous example, in early elementary classrooms and found benefits (more about that later). However, beyond research on parent-child reading in preschool (ages two to five), there is no research on how Active Reading techniques affect kids when parents use them at home past preschool.[3] Still, we can take what we know about Active Reading practices in the classroom and apply them to reading aloud at home.

Reading aloud supports kids' language development, an important part of learning to read.[4] When children start to read words on their own, when they have strong language skills, they are able to understand what they read.[5] Even as your child learns to read words on their own (also called *decoding* words), they still need to develop their ability to understand and use language.[6]

Active Reading supports your child's language development in a few ways. First, you model complex language as you read books that your child is not able to read on their own. Through listening to stories, their ability to focus on and listen to language improves. Your child learns the sentence structure and grammar that's presented in what you're reading. They also observe how you are tackling things like reading fluency and comprehension (more in Chapter 2). Then your child is encouraged to engage with the ideas in books through discussion. Your child's brain connects information from the words and pictures as you read.[7] And your child learns new words through the story and your discussion.

All this language—from listening to discussion—helps your child succeed at independent reading.[8] Your child's language ability will not influence their reading right away, but it does help them understand what they read. Specifically, in first and second grades, a child's oral language skill has an indirect effect on reading achievement as students learn to read on their own.[9]

Put another way, reading in first and second grades is more about phonics and decoding, but that changes once children master word reading and need their language skills to understand what they're reading. As children age, their language and vocabulary have more and more of an effect on what they can read and understand. One study that examined children's language and reading over time, found that children's semantic knowledge (or knowledge of words) was an important predictor of later reading skills, even more than phonemic awareness or their knowledge of sounds.[10] The kindergarten students who could remember and define many words were better readers by second grade compared with children who knew fewer words.[11]

Reading aloud also supports children's listening skills, which contribute to their ability to absorb language when they read it on their own, improving their reading comprehension and word reading.[12] In elementary school, listening comprehension becomes an important factor in children's reading comprehension,[13] which makes sense as reading is primarily a listening activity—when we read words on the page we are "hearing" them. Moreover, children who do not have strong listening comprehension skills also struggle with reading comprehension.[14]

RAISING ACTIVE READERS

Lola and her grandmother are reading The Sandwich Swap *by Queen Rania al Abdullah, a story about two friends who learn about each others' cultures through the sandwiches they bring for lunch.*

"What were the girls doing?" Lola's grandma asked, pausing midway through the book.

"They were making fun of their sandwiches," Lola replied.

"Yeah, what were they saying about the sandwiches?"

"That they were yucky."

"Mmmhmm." Lola's grandma reads a few more pages.

"Oh no, now what happened?" she asks.

"They had a food fight."

"Have you ever had a food fight in your cafeteria?"

"No, Ms. McClain wouldn't allow it."

Lola's grandma smiles and keeps reading.

"What do the girls do now?"

"They taste each other's sandwiches. And they like them."

In this example, Lola is talking just as much, if not more, than her grandmother. In Active Reading, our children are the active ones. While it is important to read with expression, add voices to characters, and be silly when the book is funny, Active Reading is about the child engaging with the story and with you in conversation. You know you're doing Active Reading right when your child is talking and thinking, when they interrupt with questions about the story (that shows you they're paying attention), and when the conversation about the book continues long after you've read the last page.

As your child grows into an independent reader, as they learn to read words by themselves, Active Reading moves from being the main way they engage with books to one of many ways. They may listen to you read aloud to them as part of a bedtime routine, or as a way to enjoy a chapter book they are not yet able to read. And, they may also read easy readers to practice their own reading skills, skim through magazines to learn about a topic they're interested in, and practice reading books they've brought home from school for homework.

The goals of Active Reading change as your child grows. Active Reading for elementary schoolers is about building vocabulary and comprehension through discussion and talking about words. It's not about teaching them how to read words, or having your child read aloud to you. While it can be part of your child's daily reading time, it should not be set to a timer or a twenty-minute requirement. Above all, Active Reading is a fun time for you to sit with your child and read together. It's an opportunity to share a favorite book from your childhood or read a new story together, and hear how your child is understanding the story and incorporating it into their own experience.

Table 1.1. What Active Reading Is and Is NOT in Grades K–3

Active Reading Is	Active Reading Is Not
• A way to engage your child with literature • A way to encourage conversation and discussion about stories and topics • Reading with (rather than to) your child • A way to support your child's vocabulary and reading comprehension • A family routine that should be enjoyable and, ideally, child driven	• Teaching your child to read • Your child reading only to you • Teaching phonics or sight words • Homework or prescribed reading (a "must-do") • A timed reading experience (for example, twenty minutes each night)

ABCS OF ACTIVE READING WITH ELEMENTARY SCHOOLERS

Active Reading can be boiled down to the ABCs: Ask questions, Build vocabulary, and make Connections. These are the things that we can do with children while we read with them that get the benefits of reading success for kids and love of reading.

A: Ask Questions

Imagine you are reading the picture book *A Sick Day for Amos McGee* by Philip Stead to your five-year-old. As you read this story about Amos, a zookeeper who misses a day of work only to have his animal friends visit him, you may ask:

- How did the animals feel when Amos did not come to work? What did they do?
- Do you think that was a good idea? Why or why not?
- How did the animals make Amos feel better?

When you ask questions about a story or topic, you're helping your child understand questions and how to answer them. You're also helping them use information from the book to answer a question, how to build their knowledge of a story and how it changes from scene to scene, and how to generate their own ideas and conclusions.

As adult readers, we constantly ask ourselves questions while we read. We may wonder what's going to happen next? We may dismay that an author killed off a character. (Why did they do that?) And we may wonder if what's being presented in a fictional story is true; would that actually happen in real life? Asking (and answering) questions helps us orient ourselves in the text, keep our place, remind us of where we have been, and helps us think about what's going to happen next.

As children grow as readers, they will practice asking questions of text and will learn to deepen their understanding of text through discussion.[15] In elementary school, students are transitioning from watching adults create meaning while reading to applying reading strategies on their own.[16] Active Reading helps children bridge those two phases: it helps children understand how adults understand text through modeling, explicit instruction, and practice with help.

B: Build Vocabulary

Reading *A Sick Day for Amos McGee*, you may talk about the concept of being an "early riser," as Amos was. You could talk about the word *amble* and how it is different from *walk*. And, you could talk about the word *concern*, and how the animals felt concerned about Amos.

When children read, they often encounter new words and must integrate new words with existing information.[17] The more words children know, or the larger their vocabulary, the stronger they are at reading comprehension.[18] Picture books and books read aloud are often ways that children learn these new words.

Through Active Reading, you'll find "rare" words, or words that your child does not know, and use the text and your conversation to help them define and understand those words. The difference between reading with younger children and older children is that younger children have smaller vocabularies, so more words are new to them, while older children will have larger vocabularies, which also means they have more word knowledge to connect new words to. Also, younger children are likely reading books that have few rare words, or rare words that repeat (the repetition of the word *lair* in *Bear Snores On* by Karma Wilson, for example) so you may find yourself talking about the same rare words again and again. Reading a longer picture book or chapter book, on the other hand, you may talk about a rare word only once and not return to it again. Reading with older children, you may also come across more rare words than you can talk through with your child without losing the thread of the story.

Even if you don't define each and every rare word you come across, building vocabulary is something that can be done, and done well, through Active Reading. It's one of the most significant and important benefits of Active Reading with children of all ages.

C: Make Connections

Connection is a big part of what makes us pick up a book and keep reading it. In *A Sick Day for Amos McGee*, your child may connect with the experience of visiting and helping a sick friend. They may connect with the theme of kindness and how we should treat each other. And they may use their knowledge of how it feels when people are kind to infer how Amos felt.

As your child reads on their own, they'll use their background knowledge, or everything they know about a topic, to understand what they read, especially when it comes to making inferences, or drawing conclusions about what they read. And they'll be looking for connections to characters, plot events, and themes to keep them reading through novels and engage them in new nonfiction books. As adult readers, we keep reading about characters we care about, and are always looking for what we read to connect with what we already know. Active Reading shows children how to make connections while reading, and how to make even more connections while reading on their own.

KEEP READING WITH ME

Active Reading is a way to engage and keep your children engaged in books as they advance from being read to, to reading on their own. As Pavon noticed, reading aloud with our children is a way to open our children up to new ideas and help them develop a love of books. In Chapter 2, I talk about how your child learns to read, and how reading aloud at home supports the work that your child does at school.

* * *

WHAT TO REMEMBER

- Reading picture books to elementary school–aged children helps children connect what they see on the page and hear in the text. Picture books are a great way to engage children with stories, themes, and topics they can't fully understand yet.
- As you read with your child, you're showing them what reading looks and sounds like, and encouraging them to interact with the book as you ask questions and talk about the book. This helps children read successfully on their own.
- When we are doing Active Reading, our children are the "active" ones as they answer questions, talk about words, and share connections they make.

- As your child grows into an independent reader, Active Reading is one of many ways they will engage with books and stories.
- The ABCs of Active Reading engage children in understanding what they read, learning and talking about "rare" words, and making inferences and other connections with what they read.

2

I Can Read on My Own!

Truth be told, I don't remember learning how to read. I remember silent reading time in Mrs. Merar's first grade classroom, and reading by flashlight at night (thinking that my parents had no idea that I was up past my bedtime). This is a common experience—you may not remember how you learned to read. Over time, reading often becomes something so simple and automatic that we don't think about it. And that's the goal. We want our children to be able to read easily, without having to stop and sound out words, unless they choose to reread something because they zoned out for a moment, or want to remember a particular sentence.

Now that you have a child who is learning to read, it's worth thinking back to your own early reading experiences:

- What do you remember about learning to read?
- What school experiences come to mind?
- What at-home experiences do you recall?
- Do you remember going to the library? What library experiences do you recall?

From your experiences:

- What do you want your own child to remember about their time learning to read?
- Which of your experiences do you want them to experience?
- What new memories do you want them to have?

Listening to your child read on their own for the first time is an amazing experience. It's a milestone on par with watching them take their first steps, or seeing them ride on a bike without training wheels. As your child goes from sounding out words to reading those first sentences aloud to laughing out loud at a joke they find in their book, there are many ways they'll show you they're an independent reader.

By the time your child starts to read, they'll have been talking for years. Spoken language develops naturally, through established circuits in the brain that are wired and ready to learn to communicate. When you sang lullabies to your infant, reassured your toddler after they fell, and explained to your preschooler where you were going while running errands, you were building important language skills. In fact, it may seem like your child picked up words and added words to their vocabulary each day without even trying. And as grammar rules fell into place, they gained understanding of how to use tenses and other rules of language and sounded more and more like adults.

In contrast, learning to read is not innate. We humans were never "born to read."[1] Each of us must be taught to read in some fashion—from children who listen to books that are read to them over and over, to children who learn to read through explicit phonics instruction in school. To learn to read even the most basic book, children must "crack the code" that helps them read words on the page. They must learn that each letter looks a certain way and represents a sound and put those sounds together to form words. And once they have cracked the code, they must layer their knowledge of word reading on top of their language skills to build meaning from what are essentially lines and scribbles. However we learn to read, if we don't have access to books, someone to read with us, and someone to help us connect spoken sounds and written words, we won't develop as readers. Reading has become one of our species' greatest accomplishments, and one that we must pass along from generation to generation through culture, experiences, and teaching.[2]

This chapter describes how children develop the ability to read, including the specific skills that children need to learn to read well, how the progression from nonreader to reader takes place, and how Active Reading fits into that development. This chapter also includes information about how you can support the work that your child is doing at school during your time at home.

WHAT IS READING?

Reading, or understanding what is written using symbols (in English, the letters of the alphabet and how those letters come together to create sound patterns and words), has long been understood as a combination of our ability to sound out (or decode) words and using our language skills to understand the words we read.[3] This formula for reading accounts for the differences between strong and weak readers; when a reader's decoding or language skills are higher, their reading comprehension will be better. And vice versa, children who have lower decoding or language skills have lower reading comprehension.[4] When a reader has poor word reading skills, they won't be able to sound out enough words to understand what they read. On the other hand, when they have weak language skills, they also won't be able to understand what they read.

Typically, children in the United States learn to read in early elementary school (kindergarten through second grade). This is when a bulk of their reading time will be spent learning letters and sound patterns and how to sound out words. Once they are skilled at reading words, typically by third or fourth grade, their underlying language skills contribute more to their reading ability as they read increasingly complex texts.[5]

For most children, sounding out words, as we cover in the next section, is fairly straightforward. Reading comprehension, or understanding what we read, is much more complex.[6] Reading comprehension takes more than just getting the words off the page; it also incorporates reader, text, and task variables.[7]

- Reader variables are those factors that the child brings to the text. This includes their background knowledge, or how much they know about what they are about to read as well as their motivation and eagerness to read the story or about the topic. (More on background knowledge in Chapter 7.)
- Text variables are features of the text that make it easier or more difficult to read:
  ○ How long are the sentences?
  ○ How many longer words are there and how often do they appear?
  ○ Is the text organized in a clear, simple way or more complex?
- Task variables relate to what the child is being asked to do with the text. For example, reading and retelling a simple fairy tale is much different than reading multiple fairy tales and synthesizing them to analyze the genre.

As you watch your child read, you may find that they read about one topic quite well while struggling to understand a text about something different, even if the second book's reading level is technically lower. For example, your child may read books with difficult words and lots of information about their favorite sport while struggling to read a simpler book about a historical period. Or you may find that your child is able to listen to and enjoy fantasy chapter books with you at home, but lacks motivation when asked to use the same books in a school project because the project isn't fun for them.

Reading is about more than getting words off the page. It has to do with language, motivation to read about the character or topic, and even how confident your child feels about what they'll do after they read. As your child enters school, they will likely progress through a sequence of learning how to read across grades K–2 that will prepare them to use text as a way to learn new information.

READING AND YOUR ELEMENTARY SCHOOLER

A lot happens between kindergarten and third grade. Your child will go from knowing the letters of the alphabet to reading entire books, and from telling stories to analyzing book plots, not to mention learning a lot about science, history, and other topics.

Even on the first day of kindergarten, you may feel like talking with your child is like having a conversation with a little adult. The average kindergartener has a vocabulary of three thousand to five thousand words and speaks in complete sentences.[8] All these words are the foundation that kindergarteners use to sound out and understand words they read.

Whether your child starts school knowing all their letters or just a few, throughout kindergarten your child will learn letters and sound patterns. They will learn that the letter *A* can say either /a/ as in "ant" or /A/ as in "cane." They'll learn that when the letters *o* and *a* are together as /oa/, they say /o/ as in "boat" and "moat." They will also learn how to sound out or decode words with short, predictable patterns, like "cat," "bet," and "cone."

In first grade, your child will have a better grasp of how to read words and will expand their knowledge of how to read individual sound patterns.[9] Students typically master the core decoding skills (phonemic awareness and phonics; Table 2.1) during kindergarten and first grade.[10] By the end of first grade, they are ready to read longer sentences and can focus on building fluency and deepening comprehension (more on this in later in this chapter). This is when Active Reading really starts to help children's comprehension as young students' vocabulary comes more into play.[11]

Starting in second grade, the relationship between decoding and vocabulary reverses and a child's ability to decode words predicts their vocabulary development.[12] As children master the ability to read words, they can use their skills to define new words using what they read. Your child will continue to learn how to sound out words, especially longer words with multiple syllables (words like *helicopter* and *pachyderm*). As they get better at sounding out words, they'll read more and more "by sight," meaning that they'll recognize words automatically without having to sound them out (as an adult reader, you are likely reading by sight right now). As you listen to your child read, you'll hear them grow from reading word by word to reading phrases and sentences, and reading with more expression. This is important because the ability to read something as they would hear it spoken aloud, or fluently, is an important part of understanding what they read.

Reading words by sight also builds comprehension by helping children shift from reading words to thinking about whole phrases and sentences because they aren't expending as much energy to decode words, leaving more "brainpower" to understand what the words are communicating. Recall that comprehension is complex, and factors such as the text, the child's knowledge about a topic, and their interest in the book all determine their comprehension. In second and third grade, children make meaning from new text by using what they already know. They may use facts about the solar system that they learned from reading with you or from a TV show they watched to understand a book about space. Or they may use their knowledge of a character in a story—the main characters, Jack and Annie, in *The Magic Tree House* series, for example—to anticipate and comprehend how those characters act in a new setting.

Third grade is an important year in American schooling, when we talk about the shift from "learning to read" to "reading to learn." This means that children are expected to have mastered the basics of reading, and can now read texts for information before they talk about them, and without as much teacher support. Also in third, fourth, and fifth grades, the text that children read becomes more complicated, with higher-level vocabulary and more complex concepts.[13] Third grade is a time when your child will become an even more independent reader. They may disappear to read for hours only to emerge wanting to tell you everything they've read about.

Unlike reading instruction in grades K–2, reading class in third grade and beyond is dedicated to talking and writing about what children learn from texts, including helping them analyze and develop their own ideas about what they've read. They will also read a variety of text genres, including fables, nonfiction, myths, and others. And they'll delve into figurative language, like metaphors and similes. This is where a lot of the conversation you've already had with your child during Active Reading will come in handy as your child can transfer the skills they learned talking about text to classroom conversations and writing.

Table 2.1. The "Big 5" of Reading

Aspect of Reading	What It Is	When Your Child Develops It
Phonemic Awareness	The ability to hear the individual sounds in words. For example, pulling apart the word /ban/ into three sounds /b/ /a/ and /n/. Also putting sounds together into words and identifying similarities and differences in words, as in rhyming.	During their preschool years
Phonics	The ability to recognize written sound patterns and read sounds together to form words. For example, reading the letters e and a together /ea/ in the words: stream, scream, and team.	Preschool through third grade
Fluency	The ability to read with an appropriate pace (not too fast and not too slow) and with accuracy and expression. This includes reading punctuation, stopping for periods, and changing your voice for question marks and exclamation points.	First grade through elementary school
Vocabulary	The knowledge of lots of different words, what they mean, and how they are used.	Throughout their life
Comprehension	The ability to understand what they read, including the basic meaning (being able to answer *what, when, where, how,* and *why* questions) and a deeper understanding (making inferences and analyzing a text).	Throughout their life

THE BIG 5: WHAT IT TAKES TO READ

When your child starts school, you'll hear about various reading skills they are working on and you may receive reports on how your child is progressing in these skills. For almost twenty years, there has been agreement that children need five core skills (the "Big 5") to read well: phonemic awareness, phonics, fluency, vocabulary, and comprehension.[14] In early elementary school, your child's reading instruction will encompass some or all of these "Big 5" each day. As your child learns to read, understanding each of these skills and how they are supported by Active Reading and through your work at home will help your child develop into a confident reader.

Phonemic Awareness

Phonemic awareness is the ability to hear sounds in words, also called *phonemes.*[15] Most words have more than one phoneme, or sound. For example,

the word *cat* has three sounds, /c/ /a/ /t/. The word *boat* also has three phonemes /b/ /oa/ and /t/. Phonemic awareness, and knowing the sounds that
make up the English language, is a precursor to reading words. Along with
knowing the letters of the alphabet (letter knowledge), phonemic awareness
is one of two key skills that have an important influence on a child's reading
in the first two years of school.[16] Active Reading with younger children (as
outlined in the book about Active Reading with younger children, *Read with
Me*)[17] helps develop young children's phonemic awareness.

Phonics

Phonics, or sounding out words, is what we typically think of when we think
about word reading. Most children need some explicit, systematic phonics
instruction to learn to read words and read well.[18] This means that sounds and
the letter or letters that make up those sounds are taught from the letters we
use most often (m, s, e) to those we use the least (z, q) and in a direct manner.

As a parent, you should expect some explicit phonics instruction in school to
support your child's reading development (see textbox on the following page).
The goal of phonics instruction is automaticity, or that a reader can look at a
letter or word and read it automatically (or by sight). This frees up space in the
brain to focus on meaning. Put another way, when we can read and understand
words automatically, our brains are able to work most efficiently, and free up
space to use for making sense of what we read, including higher-order thinking.[19]

Active Reading is removed from phonemic awareness and phonics. The
purpose of Active Reading is not to teach phonics, but to build the language,
vocabulary, and comprehension skills that children need to understand what
they read once they have mastered phonics.

Fluency

Fluency is the ability to read words and phrases clearly, at an appropriate
pace, with expression. In many ways, you know fluent reading when you
hear it; think of how an audiobook sounds. When a child can read fluently,
they are able to read at a pace that allows them to "hear" what they read and
with expression that provides meaning. As children develop fluency, they
will increase their reading rate, or the speed of reading, and they'll develop
improved expression. They will also advance from reading word by word to
reading phrases and sentences, which helps them understand what they are
reading. Active Reading does not teach fluency directly, but it is a time to
model fluent reading and, as your child grows, an opportunity to have your
child read to you, which develops their fluency as well.

Whole Language vs. Phonics: Is There a Debate?

In 2000, the National Reading Panel (NRP), a group of reading researchers, published a report about how children learn to read and the type of instruction that children need to become strong readers.[1] The report was based on a review of hundreds of research studies.

Prior to the NRP report, experts debated how to teach reading. Some experts encouraged a whole language approach, while others promoted explicit phonics instruction. In the whole language approach, reading was seen as a natural activity and the best way to teach children to read was to read to them and allow them to have time with books. Proponents of phonics instruction argued that children needed instruction in how words were put together through lessons that taught letters and sounds.

The NRP report was clear: children benefit from explicit phonics instruction, and when children receive explicit instruction, the vast majority learn to read. Since then explicit phonics instruction has become an important part of literacy instruction in schools. Of course, your child should have lots of different experiences with books and print in class each day, including read-aloud, the opportunity to read by themselves or to a partner, and practice with individual words and sound patterns. However, for reading researchers the debate is over and explicit phonics instruction should be part of every child's reading day. As a parent, you can ask your child's teacher or school:

- How do you teach phonics and word reading?
- What programs or approaches are used?
- How do those programs or approaches incorporate explicit, systematic phonics instruction?

There are a variety of programs that teach phonics well, the key is to incorporate clear phonics instruction for every reader.

Note

1. National Reading Panel, 2000.

Vocabulary

A child's vocabulary is, simply put, the number of words they know. A child's semantic knowledge, or their knowledge of word definitions and their ability to recall words, is an important predictor of later reading skill.[20] Specifically, kindergarteners' understanding of words was so important that it was a predictor of their reading comprehension in second grade.[21]

However, vocabulary is about more than being able to rattle off the definitions of words; it's also about having words at the ready, to use to describe what we're feeling, explain our thoughts, and to justify our opinions. That requires using words in lots of different ways, including discussing books.

When you read to your child, you're exposing them to lots of words they wouldn't hear otherwise. Vocabulary is an important outcome of Active Reading. Reading with children develops their vocabulary in important ways, both expanding the number of words a child knows and their understanding of those words (more on vocabulary in Chapter 5).

Comprehension

Comprehension, or understanding what we read, is the ultimate goal of reading—what good is sounding out words on a page if you can't understand what they mean? It's also a very complex aspect of reading. Understanding what we read draws on our word reading, fluency, thinking skills, language, and more.[22]

Active Reading is an important way to develop comprehension because it encourages asking questions and talking about the text, both of which are important for understanding what we read.[23] In elementary school, students are transitioning from learning how we understand what we read by watching adults read to applying those strategies and ways of thinking to texts they read on their own.[24] Active Reading helps children both understand how you understand what you're reading as you engage in conversation and ask questions, and encourages them to build their own meaning.[25]

Active Reading builds children's working memory, or ability to hold lots of information in their minds at once.[26] As we start reading a novel, for example, we'll hold character names, setting details, plot events, in our working memory until we can make sense of what's happening in the story; then we'll package each scene into the larger narrative as we move through the story, building an ever-larger store of information about a text or topic (more on this later in this chapter).

LANGUAGE: THE FOUNDATION FOR READING

Grace, who is six years old and new to reading on her own, is reading the now classic Frog and Toad Together *by Arnold Lobel. In the story, Toad makes a list of things that he has to do that day (wake up, go see Frog, take a walk), but when the list gets blown away, Toad isn't sure what to do. In the end, he writes, "Go to sleep" in the dirt, crosses it off, and falls asleep. Grace chuckles. "He forgot to eat supper," she says, delighted.*

As she reads *Frog and Toad Together*, Grace is sounding out words and reading sentences; she's also using her knowledge of language to understand the sequence and funny parts of the story—that Toad cannot figure out what to do when the list flies away and that he only remembers to fall asleep. She's developing an understanding of the story that goes beyond recalling the basic sequence of events.

Reading words and using knowledge of language to understand what we read is the basic way to look at reading comprehension.[27] A child's ability to listen and understand and produce language is an important part of their ability to read. Spoken or oral language encompasses semantic skills (word knowledge, the ability to understand and express themselves using language), the rules of grammar (syntactic awareness), narrative structure or how stories are structured, and knowledge about lots of different topics.[28] Since children must translate words on the page into language they can "hear" and understand, their knowledge of language is a critical skill that they must develop well into their school-aged years.[29]

As mentioned earlier, younger children's oral language skills are not as strongly correlated or connected to reading ability.[30] However, as children progress and start reading more complex texts, their ability to understand and carry meaning across a text depends on their language skill. Over time, their language ability becomes increasingly important for their success as readers.[31] You may see this as your child processes information out loud during or after reading. They may ask more questions when you read to them, or they may read an article about a topic and then talk about it until they seem to have solidified all the information they need before moving on to the next topic.

We think about language in two ways. The first is expressive language, or the language we use to express ourselves. And, there is receptive language, or our ability to understand the language that we hear or read. Both are important and Active Reading is a proven way to improve children's receptive and expressive language skills.[32] Put another way, listening comprehension (receptive language) is important for reading success.[33] In fact, a child's listening comprehension skills predicted word identification skills for students in elementary school who struggled to learn to read.[34] And the key to improving children's expressive language is that the children are asked to respond to what they're read (the *A* of Active Reading; see Chapter 4).

ACTIVE READING AND THE HOME-SCHOOL CONNECTION

If you have time to do *one thing* with your child after school (and dinner and homework)—read with them. We know that how parents are involved in their child's education has an influence on their child's academic development.[35] As a parent, you have your attention and time pulled in many different directions and you can support your child's school in a myriad of ways. Not that helping your child bake cookies for a fund-raiser and chaperoning field trips aren't important, but the best way to support your child at home is to read with them (and it can be done in addition to field trips and fund-raising). It's a direct connection; when parents read to children at home, children's literacy improves.[36] Reading to your child at home is one of the things you can do at home that will carry over into school.[37]

How Do Parents Contribute to Reading Success?

As a parent, you contribute to your child's success in many ways. Yes, family background does have an effect on children. The area you live in, your family background, and other aspects are factors that influence your child.

Put another way, we know that when a child comes from a higher-income family with parents who have had more education, they are more likely to do well in school.[38] Some of these aspects are fixed, and you likely can't do a whole lot about them—your education level and family background are probably already established. However, what you do when you read with your child matters. The good news is when it comes to building reading skills, what parents do at home is vitally important and can contribute to a child's ultimate success in school. What you do at home can even be more influential than some of those other fixed factors.

When parents engaged children in Active Reading, children developed stronger reading skills.[39] Specifically, when parents talked about what they read with their children, described pictures, and helped their child understand by paraphrasing, making connections, and extending stories with more conversation, their children did better in reading comprehension. What we as parents do at home matters, and with limited time after school and on weekends, focusing on conversation and Active Reading is time well spent.

More Ways to Help Your Child with Reading at Home

Active Reading is a powerful way to support your growing reader. Here are other ways that you can infuse reading into your home in the early elementary years:

- "Sell" reading to your child by presenting it as something fun that you get to do together, rather than a "have to do" or "should do."

- Take time to enjoy reading a magazine or book you want to read! Tell your child about what you're reading or what you learned.
- Fill your house with lots of different types of reading material. Recipe books, magazines, and catalogues are all fun things for your child to pick up and read.
- Encourage activities that require reading, such as cooking (using a recipe), researching something that you're interested in (using online resources), or following directions to build a tree house (using a manual).
- Have a set time when everyone in your family stops everything and reads.
- Write notes to your child. You could write a note about your day, or a note of encouragement. In your note, encourage them to write you back.
- Spark new interests by taking your child to a museum or local event. Then write down their questions and see how you can research either online or at the library and read to find the answers.

LET'S READ!

Watching your child grow into a successful reader occurs over the course of years, and will happen at school and home. At home, Active Reading is the most powerful thing you can do to ensure that your child is gaining the vocabulary, language, and comprehension skills they need to be successful. In Chapter 3, we'll focus on what you need to provide your child with lots of Active Reading . . . lots of books!

* * *

WHAT TO REMEMBER

- There are five important skills that come together to create strong readers: phonemic awareness, phonics, fluency, vocabulary, and comprehension. Children start developing these "Big 5" skills before school (when they are playing rhyming games, for example), learn them during school, and build them throughout their lives (for example, as they develop their vocabulary into adulthood).
- Language is an important factor in reading comprehension; when children have strong language skills, both what they understand (receptive) and can express (expressive), they are better able to understand what they read.
- In the early elementary grades, your child's vocabulary predicts their word decoding abilities. However, this shifts in second grade, when

their ability to decode words predicts vocabulary development as they start learning more words from text and not from conversation or reading aloud.

- In terms of building reading skill, what adults do at home is vital and can be more important than other factors, like where you live or your education background.
- Reading at home with kids is a powerful way to use your time at home to have an effect on your child's school success.

3

Books, Books, Books

Building a Library for a Growing Reader

Monica McMahon has a clear memory of her mom reading aloud *Where the Wild Things Are* by Maurice Sendak and later *The Little Prince* by Antoine de Saint-Exupery. When it came time to start reading novels with her own son, Jude, age five, she reached for *The Little Prince* because she wanted him to have that same experience. Unfortunately, Jude was not interested in *The Little Prince* at all.

Disappointed, but not deterred, McMahon recalled that Jude liked stories that made him scared. "I noticed that he liked to be thrilled or scared when he read," she says. She tried *James and the Giant Peach* by Roald Dahl and paired it with the movie to boost his understanding. They read it in bits and pieces, a few pages or a chapter at a time. And, to her delight, Jude followed along and enjoyed the story. After that, they read other Roald Dahl books that had scary moments: *Matilda, The Witches, Charlie and the Chocolate Factory*, and others.

Thinking about the books you choose for your child:

- How do you choose them?
- What about your child's current development or interests drives the books you select?
- Are there books from your own childhood that you would like to read with your child?
- When you've finished one book, what resources do you use to find the next book to read?

With twin six-year-old boys and their five-year-old brother, Erin Pavon's evening reading can be all humor and superheroes. They read titles like *Splat the Cat* by Rob Scotton, *The Day the Crayons Came Home* by Drew Daywalt, *Dragons Love Tacos* by Adam Rubin, and compilations of Marvel and Star Wars five-minute stories. The titles may not be what you'd consider great literature, but they are books her kids return to night after night. That's the goal of an Active Reading library for your child—to find books that will stand the test of time for your children's development, interests, and personality, including their sense of humor.

Pavon's shelves are filled with humorous picture books; imagine your child's reading corner. Enough pillows and stuffed animals for a young reader to get lost in. Books—favorite picture books, thick chapter books, and all the books from a favorite series—line a bookshelf or fill bins on the floor. Or perhaps your child has taken over a cozy armchair that is the perfect size for them to drape both legs over, dangling as they read book after book from a stack on the floor.

Your child's home reading experience, where and how they sit, and how they store and organize their books can look any number of ways. The most important thing may be that they have books at all. There are lots of advantages that come with having a shelf or a few bins of their own books at home.[1] In fact, raising a reader may be as simple as providing them with a small collection (imagine one shelf-full) of books that evolves as they do.

Put another way, regardless of a family's income level or the parents' education (two common indicators that are used to predict how well a child will do in school), when a child from any home has more books available to them, they do better. All in all, the evidence is clear: books benefit all kids.

When your child starts reading on their own, their progress develops slowly. They'll read simple, repetitive books that give them lots of practice in how to sound out words. These easy readers don't have a lot of new vocabulary and the stories are not complex. Think *Frog and Toad* by Arnold Lobel and *Little Bear* by Else Minarik. During this time, reading aloud becomes an important way that your child will engage with longer and more complex stories, new genres, and informational books that feed their curiosity about topics they are interested in.

Also, in their early years, reading may be a challenging task for your child. Cuddling up to listen to a story may remain a way for them to relax into a book. Without having to put work into sounding out words, they can sit back and enjoy the story, keeping and building a love of reading. And even with lots of Active Reading, there will be times when your child just wants to hear the story read aloud, without breaks for questions or conversation (that's okay!).

As your child grows, their bookshelf will change as well. It may have already shifted from board books to picture books. The next change may be to easy readers and chapter books, and eventually novels. Even as your child starts reading on their own, picture books and chapter books you read together should still make up a portion of their book selection. So having books at home helps kids become readers. But which books? How can we get books that "grow" with our kids? What books are best for Active Reading with early elementary schoolers? And how do we stock home libraries with so many books without breaking the budget?

The shelves of books that provide such benefits can come from trips to the library, presents from family and friends, used book sales, and any number of other sources. When your child starts school, they may bring home books to read from the classroom or school library. Wherever the books come from, it's important to keep your home library well stocked, and provide a wide variety of reading experiences.

This chapter covers the ideas behind building a library that encourages your child to read wide and deep, the genres of books that make for a robust Active Reading experience, why and how to incorporate diversity into your child's home library, and why to focus on "tree books" over e-books. This chapter also provides information about how your child's independent reading will develop and what you should know about the reading levels they will progress through as they learn to read.

ACTIVE READING WIDE AND DEEP

Adia, age eight, brings home a stack of books on her favorite topic: science. She's read fiction and nonfiction about science. She's read Ada Twist, Scientist *by Andrea Beaty so often she can recite it. She's read the early chapter book series* Zoey *and* Sassafras *by Asia Citro from start to finish. Her father indulges her love of science with some books about scientists, and lots of* Magic School Bus *books, but during their Active Reading time each night, her dad reads books with female heroines.* Matilda *by Roald Dahl,* Pippi Longstocking *by Astrid Lindgren, Lucy and Susan in* The Chronicles of Narnia *series by C. S. Lewis. This variety of reading experiences gives Adia a deep knowledge of science, as well as a wide range of experiences with the novel genre and the different types of female characters.*

Just as you want your child to "eat the rainbow" as they fill their plate with fruits, vegetables, and other healthy foods, you'll want your child to have experience with a wide range of story and books types, genres, authors, characters, and language. When children read widely, they gain lots of knowledge about many different things, and are exposed to lots of different authors, stories, and characters. This provides them with a starting point to read more about any of those topics on their own. For example, reading aloud *The Lion, the Witch and the Wardrobe* by C. S. Lewis, *The Hobbit* by J. R. R. Tolkien, and *Aru Shah and the End of Time* by Roshani Chokshi teaches children about the genre of fantasy and how to enjoy and understand worlds entirely created by the author. They don't have to love fantasy to understand and enjoy the genre.

As another example, reading a lot of different nonfiction books, like *The Magic School Bus* books, *National Geographic Kids* books, and the *DK Eyewitness* book series, will offer introductions to topics from the human body to weather systems. Even if your child doesn't take to each topic, knowing a little about each one will help them build a foundation of knowledge they can build on as they read about other topics and even stories. For example, knowing about the beach and ocean helps your child understand stories that are set along the shore, even if it just supports their ability to visualize the setting.

In addition to reading widely, you'll also want your child to delve deeply into books about one topic or one genre of story. This is called *deep reading*. Deep reading occurs when a child falls in love with a topic, genre, author, or character and reads everything they can get their hands on. The benefit is that they gain knowledge and learn to love and truly connect with that story or character. For example, children who are interested in space may read about space in general (*National Geographic Kids* series *Little Kids First Big Book of Space* by Catherine D. Hughes and *13 Planets: The Latest View of the Solar System* by David Aguilar). They may also read stories that have space events as a plot (*Meteor!* by Patricia Polacco) and they may want to read about famous people associated with space (*Mae among the Stars* by Roda Ahmed or *Reaching for the Moon* by Buzz Aldrin). All this reading teaches them the facts and vocabulary about space, how space has affected people, and how we've affected space. When children read deep on one topic, they learn concepts and facts about the topic, and they also learn vocabulary and gain experience reading lots of different text structures (more in Chapter 7).

YOUR CHILD'S READING "DIET"

When your child was a toddler or preschooler, choosing books for them may have involved picking picture books that had rich illustrations, interesting stories, and lots of language. Now that your child is older, choosing books to read aloud means choosing books that expand their knowledge and experience by introducing them to new authors, genres, or information, or choosing books that challenge their lengthening attention span as they start to follow stories through an entire novel.

Appendix A contains a list of books that are ideal for Active Reading, but these general guidelines will help you choose books that create a complete reading diet that will engage and challenge your child. In addition to picture books, fill your child's shelves with illustrated chapter books, myths, fairy tales, folktales, your favorite titles, books that your child gravitates toward, poetry, nonfiction, books that are aspirational for your child, and popular titles.

Illustrated Chapter Books

The first chapter book that I read with my oldest daughter was *Mercy Watson* by Kate DiCamillo. This series, about a pig living with Mr. and Mrs. Watson, who gets into lots of mischief in her quest to secure more of her favorite treat (hot buttered toast), was a great first chapter book. The *Mercy Watson* books are heavily illustrated, allowing my daughter to gain knowledge from the pictures as well as the story, and have enough elements of chapter books to make it feel different than a picture book.

Illustrated chapter books, like *Mercy Watson* and other titles like the *Yasmin* books by Saadia Faruqi, *Zoey and Sassafrass* by Asia Citro, and the *EllRay Jakes* series by Sally Warner, are a wonderful transition from the world of picture books to chapter books. The chapters are short with pictures throughout, and the pictures and words combine to help your child create meaning.[2] Often, these books come in a series so you can read multiple stories about one character, which provides conversation about how characters have traits that stay the same from story to story, and what changes in each book.

Myths, Fairy Tales, and Folktales

Reading aloud is one way to expose kids to the rich language and stories that we find in fairy tales, Greek myths, and other stories. These are stories that everyone knows that cut across culture and language, including Cinderella, Noah and the Flood, Anansi stories, King Arthur stories, Aesop's fables, and even superhero stories. These are foundational, meaning that other stories often take characters, themes, and references from these tales. Knowing about the archetypes and events of these stories lend meaning to other, modern books.

It's likely that, while your child will enjoy these classic stories, they won't be able to read the original or retellings on their own because these stories are often written in language that is from a different era and the retellings keep lots of the rich, complex language. Good examples of classic stories you can read with your child include *Rapunzel* by Paul Zelinsky, *Hansel and Gretel* by Susan Jeffers, the *Knights' Tales* series by Gerald Morris, and the fairy-tale retellings by Cynthia Rylant.)

Your Favorites

Reading aloud to your child is a great time to expose your child to books that you loved as a child. Sharing favorite books that your parents read to you, or that you read on your own, can help you connect with your child and open conversations about what the stories meant to you. Your child may not have the same reaction or connection to a book, but you can share what you liked about the book and show them what it looks like when a book has an effect on someone. One thing to note, as McMahon learned, is that your child's perfect age for a story may be different than your own. So, if you open your favorite novel only to find that your child isn't interested, put it back for a year or so until they're ready to try it again.

Your Child's Perfect Fit

Reading aloud is also an opportunity to create new favorites. As your child's personality evolves, you can bring in books that suit them best. Books that resonated with their sense of humor and spark their interests help them see themselves as readers as they connect to the humor, topic, or character. Even if your child's interests are far from your own (I'm willing to guess that your interests don't include bodily substances and farts, even though your second grader may find the topic hilarious), reading *Captain Underpants* by Dav Pilkey and *Stink!* By Megan McDonald can be a way to share a laugh. Also, this shows children how their interests are represented in the books they read, and that there truly is a book for everybody.

Poetry

Poetry can be powerful for young readers. Poetry is best read aloud so young readers can hear how the words should sound. Reading poetry aloud also helps you engage kids in the feelings that language can evoke. Collections by Shel Silverstein (*Where the Sidewalk Ends* and *A Light in the Attic*) and Jack Prelutsky (*The New Kid on the Block* and *Something Big Has Been Here*) as well as collections of poetry specifically for kids (*Honey, I Love* by Eloise Greenfield and *My Village: Rhymes from around the World* by Danielle Wright) are good introductions to the genre.

Nonfiction

As discussed in the section on reading deeply, nonfiction builds important background knowledge. Nonfiction books about sharks, dinosaurs, outer space, and anything else your child is interested in, will have vocabulary words they can't necessarily read, but want to know. Reading these books together allows you to teach them those words. It also allows you to show your child how to use nonfiction books, which, with a glossary, table of contents, and other reference points, can be different than a straight-through fiction read. And it allows you to ask questions about a topic and find answers together (more on reading nonfiction in Chapter 7).

Books beyond Their Years

For young readers, books can be aspirational, meaning that children are always looking to what they can read next. When they are reading easy readers, they'll be looking to read that first chapter book. When they read a chapter book, they may be eyeing the *Harry Potter* series or a book that their older sibling or friend is reading. Reading aloud can help children see what's coming up as you read increasingly long and challenging, more "grown-up" chapter books with them. Reading books like *The Lion, the Witch and the Wardrobe* by C. S. Lewis, *The Unicorn Rescue Society* by Adam Gidwitz, *Aru Shah and the End of Time* by Roshani Chokshi, and others can motivate children and help them see how reading can be an ever-present part of their life. Also, knowing that your child's listening comprehension will be more advanced than their reading comprehension until middle school, exposing them to stories that challenges their listening comprehension is a great way to keep them engaged in novels as they develop the reading skills to tackle them on their own.[3]

The Latest, Greatest Books

There was a time when every kid was carrying around a copy of *Harry Potter* by J. K. Rowling. Then it was *Diary of a Wimpy Kid* by Jeff Kinney. At the start of every new popular series, or when a book becomes a movie and everyone is talking about it, there will be kids who desperately want to experience those stories even though the actual text is beyond them. Provided that the topics are age appropriate, reading stories that everyone else is reading helps your child participate in the larger reading culture, which can be especially important for young readers in school.

Table 3.1. Types of Books for Your Home Library

Type of Book	Description	Examples
Illustrated Chapter Books	Chapter books with longer stories than picture books and with lots of illustrations to be read aloud or for children to read on their own with some support	*Mercy Watson* by Kate DiCamillo *Princess in Black* by Shannon Hale *Dory Fantasmagory* by Abby Hanlon *Yasmin* series by Saadia Faruqui *King and Kayla* books by Dori Butler
Your Favorite Books	Books that you loved to listen to as a child	*Charlotte's Web* by E. B. White *Matilda* by Roald Dahl *Bud, Not Buddy* by Christopher Paul Curtis
Your Child's Perfect Fit	Books that your child finds funny, engaging, and inherently interesting	If your child loves silly humor, books like *Dragons Love Tacos* by Adam Rubin or *Captain Underpants* by Dav Pilkey could be good reads. For a child who loves unicorns and fairies, *The Rainbow Fairy* books by Daisy Meadows would be a good read.
Myths, Fairy Tales, and Fantasy	Classic stories that have stood the test of time and are referenced in other stories a lot	Anansi the Spider stories by Eric Kimmel *Rapunzel* by Paul Zelinsky *A Child's Introduction to Greek Mythology* by Heather Alexander *The Knights' Tales* series by Gerald Morris
Poetry	Collections of poetry that engage children in the rhythm, rhyme, and fun of thinking about poems	*Where the Sidewalk Ends* by Shel Silverstein *Honey, I Love* by Eloise Greenfield
Nonfiction	Books about lots of different topics, including various genres of nonfiction (biographies, etc.)	*DK Eyewitness* books *National Geographic Kids* books *Magic School Bus* books
Books beyond Their Years	Novels and stories that are a step more advanced than what they're reading now, so they can see what's coming	Novels like *The Hobbit* by J. R. R. Tolkien and *Esperanza Rising* by Pam Munoz Ryan are books that children may enjoy listening to but cannot read on their own yet.
The Latest and Greatest	Series or stories that all the kids are talking about	*Harry Potter* by J. K. Rowling *Diary of a Wimpy Kid* by Jeff Kinney

WINDOWS AND MIRRORS: CULTIVATING DIVERSITY AND EMPATHY THROUGH BOOKS

There is an emotional quality to reading; we read a story and we feel the sadness of a scene. We ache for a character's loss. We are sickened by the description of an injustice. We feel happy when a character succeeds. In this way, books build empathy by teaching children about the world they live in; that includes experiences that are like their own and experiences that are far from anything they will ever experience. (Active Reading and building empathy is covered in Chapter 6.)

It's important for all children to see themselves, and others, in stories they read. There is currently a lack of diversity in children's books.[4] In 2018, 50 percent of characters in children's books were White. Twenty-seven percent were animals. The rest were children from non-White backgrounds (10 percent African American, 7 percent Asian/Pacific Islander, 5 percent Latino, and 1 percent American Indian).[5] Although this is an improvement from 2015, when 73 percent of characters were White, it is still concerning that children's books do not reflect the world that our children are growing up in, with our increasing diversity and need to understand different perspectives.

Using reading and books as a way to improve our children's understanding of themselves and others, we can think of books as "windows" or "mirrors" for our children. They are windows in that they show children another experience or way of being and mirrors when they reflect our children's own experiences.[6] It's important for kids to have reading experiences that provide both.

Books as Windows

Reading a book provides an experience, so when children read about a person or experience that is very different from their own, they are able to, even in some slight way, have that other experience. In this way, reading books about people who are different from us reduces stereotypes and distance.[7] That means that, through reading, children can gain knowledge and build empathy for experiences as diverse as what it's like to be a refugee in *Lost and Found Cat: The True Story of Kunkush's Incredible Journey* by Doug Kuntz or being friends with someone much different than you in *The Other Side* by Jacqueline Woodson. Books about experiences that are much different than the ones your child has can kindle important discussions about how we are different and similar.

Books as Mirrors

On the other hand, when children see themselves represented in books through characters that look and have experiences like them, they gain ideas about who they may become or grow up to be.[8] It's validating to read about a character that's just like us, or to see how a character went through an experience that sounds like our own life. Even an experience as simple as reading about how Jabari overcame his fear of jumping off the high dive in *Jabari Jumps* by Gaia Cornwall can be enough to make books relevant for a child.

You can find books that reflect your child's experience, and give them glimpses into other experiences through your local library as well as through purchasing books. The thing to keep in mind is how the experiences that your child has with books reflects the diversity of the world they'll experience outside your home.

BOOKS THEY READ ON THEIR OWN

As children start to read on their own, their experiences with reading will expand. Once they are not reliant on you to read the words anymore, they'll be able to engage with easy readers, simple chapter books, and eventually full novels on their own. As with many other things in parenting, providing diversity is key. Children should spend some time reading books that they can access on their own; you may hear of these as *leveled readers*.

Leveled Readers

Leveled readers are books that are categorized and organized according to how difficult they are to read. This provides one way to organize books in classrooms, though not all schools organize books in this way. In general, the higher the letter or number on a book, the more difficult it is, meaning that the words are longer and more complex and there is more of a story to follow. A child will start to read books that are simple with patterns ("I see the hat. I see the dog.") and progress to reading books with longer sentences and more complex stories, like the classics *Frog and Toad* by Arnold Lobel and *Little Bear* by Else Minarik. After that, children will start to read chapter books (like *Junie B. Jones* by Barbara Park or *Stink!* by Megan McDonald) with slightly more complex stories, longer chapters, and fewer pictures. And finally they will graduate to novels, with very few, if any, pictures and stories that can get very complicated.

In school, your child will likely be assessed to determine how well they read. Your child's teacher can use that information to select books that they can likely read without too much difficulty. They will also use this information to choose books that can challenge them and provide them opportunity to practice word patterns that they are learning. Children will work through a range of levels across a school year, and to that end, a range of typical starting points (see Table 3.2).

Your child may spend time reading independently using leveled readers in school each day. This is important for practice. Children need lots of practice to become strong readers, and reading books at their level will help them gain accuracy and comprehension in independent reading while they work to gain skills that will help them read even more difficult books.

If leveled readers are a part of your child's book diet, or the various ways they engage with books, how you read leveled readers is different than how you'll do Active Reading with more complex picture books and chapter books. When your child brings home a leveled reader, encourage them to read it to you and ask them questions about what they read. They may need to read it a few times before they can answer questions or retell the story, and that's okay. If your child makes a mistake while reading with you, that's okay too. When this happens, wait a few seconds to give them time to figure it out. If they don't read the word on their own, tell your child the correct word and move on. The point of reading with your child is to enjoy the experience and have fun. If you are looking for more leveled readers for your home library, look for books that are a level or two below their in-school reading level, so they will have mastered the skills that the book requires.

Another way to help children choose books that are a good fit is to have them read the first fifty or so words (the first page of a chapter book or first pages of an easy reader) and if they struggle with five or more words, that book may not be a good fit because they're not able to read enough words on their own to maintain their understanding of the story. If that's the case, put the book aside or put it on a list of books that they'd like to read, and choose another one.

My First Chapter Books

Your child's first chapter book is an important milestone. It's when they've shifted from reading simple books to books with weight, a story, a spine. Chapter books help young readers build stamina as they read stories that require them to read over multiple sessions (more on chapter books in Chapter 8).

Chapter books for children in grades 2 and 3 often come in series, like *The Magic Tree House* series by Mary Pope Osborn, the *Junie B. Jones* books by Barbara Park, the *Sofia Martinez* books by Jacqueline Jules, and the *Lulu* books (*Lulu and the Rabbit Next Door* and others) by Hilary McKay, among others.

Table 3.2.   Reading Levels by Grade Level

This table provides an overview of the leveled reading levels that children will read at across grades K–3. Use the table to find books for your child to read independently.

Grade	Guided Reading Levels (Fountas and Pinnell)
Kindergarten	A
	B
	C
	D
Grade 1	E
	F
	G
	H
Grades 1 and 2	I
Grade 2	J
	K
	L
Grades 2 and 3	M
Grade 3	N
	O
	P

This is wonderful because your child can build knowledge about a setting or characters and take that knowledge from book to book. When your child reads series, they carry the information about the characters and setting from book to book, making the series feel like a comfortable read from the first page.

TREE BOOKS VERSUS E-BOOKS

The conversation about how best to read books and whether to read on paper ("tree books") or tablets ("e-books") is a recent one. It's only in the last few decades that books have become available on screens. The benefit of e-readers is clear; being able to carry an entire library of stories and books in our back pocket is amazing. However, for young children, who are learning how to read and think about what they are reading, it is worth giving up shelf space for paper books. Overall, tree books are still preferable over e-books.

How well our brains can handle reading on e-readers is a new topic for research. And the effect that e-readers have on children's brains, which are still developing, is particularly new. So we don't know a lot about it. Specifically, we don't know whether reading on screens develops the same level of attention and processing as print books, and how the quality of attention and thinking about reading changes as we read on screens versus on paper.[9]

We do know how our brains comprehend text on the paper page, and we know how beneficial it is for children to engage with words on the page. We do not have as clear an understanding of how our brains engage with text on screen. Once children have the skills necessary to engage in deep reading on their own, they can bring those skills to an e-reader, just as we adults do. But until then, my bias is, admittedly, toward tree books.

BOOKS MATTER

In short: books matter. Children need to read a lot. They need to read lots of different types of books. Even a shelf full of books can make a huge difference in a child's love of reading and success in school. Active Reading provides a robust range of experiences with literature as children learn to read on their own. Chapter 4 is about the *A* of Active Reading: Asking questions.

* * *

WHAT TO REMEMBER

- Children should have experiences reading both wide and deep.
  - Wide reading occurs when a child reads lots of different genres and about many different topics.
  - Deep reading occurs when a child reads everything they can find about one topic.
- As your child starts to read on their own, providing a "reading diet" of different genres and stories helps them develop as a reader and shows them all the ways they can connect with books. There are lots of different types of books to share with them: illustrated picture books, poetry, nonfiction, myths, fairy tales and fantasy stories, and general-interest chapter books.
- Books are a way to share characters and experiences that expand and extend our children's understanding of how the world works, and how others experience the world. One way to think about that is to think about books serving as windows and mirrors.
  - When books are windows, they show children experiences that are different from their own.

- ◦ When books are mirrors, they allow children to read about experiences that are similar to their own.
- Children need lots of practice reading to become strong readers. Leveled readers are books that are organized by how difficult they are to read, so children can read a book that they are likely to have success with as they practice. When your child reads a leveled reader to you, encourage them to read and ask questions about what they read to you.
- Chapter books are an important milestone in reading. They help children build stamina and read more complex stories.
- We know how our brains work with and understand print books, but much less is known about how our brains interact with digital books. Even with the benefits of e-readers, reading "tree books" is still preferable for children.

4

Ask Questions

Each Kindness by Jacqueline Woodson is a picture book about how one child reacts when a new girl, who looks like she does not have as much money as the rest of the class, joins the classroom. Reading *Each Kindness* to my kindergarten-aged daughter, I wanted her to think about how she could be kind and inclusive. I asked:

- What does the girl [the narrator] do when Maya comes to school?
- What could the girl have done differently?
- Why do you think Maya is bringing the toys from home?
- Why do you think Maya is jumping by herself?
- How does the girl feel at the end? What could she do next time there is a new girl at school?

Asking these questions sparked conversation about how to include children, without lecturing.

Thinking about a conversation you had with your child recently, about a book or general topic:

- What questions did you ask?
- What did you learn from your child?
- What do you think your child took away from the conversation?
- As your child gets older, what questions can you ask now that could spark even more conversation?

As Erin Pavon read *Dragons Love Tacos 2* by Adam Rubin with her boys (twins, age six, and their brother, age five), they talked about time machines. "What is a time machine?" Logan, one of her boys, asked. Pavon explained and Logan followed up with a series of questions: Is it real? What would happen if you were in one? His initial questions prompted a fifteen-minute discussion about time machines before they got back to reading the story. It's these conversations about stories that make Active Reading so powerful. They build language and comprehension skills, even if the topic is time machines in a book about dragons and tacos.

Active Reading hinges on the *A*: Ask questions. During Active Reading, we want children to think about what we are reading. Asking questions is how we invite them to engage and become "active." Asking questions in Active Reading is about more than peppering kids with questions; it's about asking questions so that we can have a conversation about what we're reading together, to make the experience of reading aloud with your child into a time to learn more about what your child is thinking and wondering.

Often, we think about questions as a means to an end, as a way to find out what our child knows or has done. You may ask your child hundreds of questions throughout the day (What did you do at school? What do you want to eat? Did you brush your teeth?). But questions are also an opportunity to see how your child understands their world and what they are thinking. In this lens, even a simple question—What do you want for dinner?—is an invitation to think forward in time about what you're craving, think strategically about what's in the fridge, or assess how you feel about the effort to cook or order food. When we ask questions while we read, we're inviting children to think about the story in new ways and to engage with us in conversation. Ultimately, we want to close a book with a new idea or understanding because of the questions we asked and the conversation we had.

This chapter covers why we ask questions while reading, how to ask questions, and how to help children think deeply about what they read through answering questions. It will focus on reading and asking questions about fiction stories. (Nonfiction is covered in Chapter 7.)

THE IMPORTANCE OF CONVERSATION

Officer Buckle and Gloria by Peggy Rathmann is a story about a police officer who is obsessed with safety tips but is painfully dull in his presentations. That is, until Gloria, a dog, joins him and makes his acts more engaging for the audience by acting out Officer Buckle's lectures. Officer Buckle's message is getting through and safety is improving, but then he realizes that

Gloria has been performing behind his back during performances and feels betrayed. At the end of the story, Officer Buckle realizes that Gloria was trying to help and they remain friends.

"What do you think Officer Buckle learned?" Dad asks six-year-old Clara, after they finish the story.

"To be patient with each other," says Clara.

"What makes you think that?"

"Because Officer Buckle had to be patient with Gloria when he learned that she was doing tricks and he didn't know."

"Hmm, okay, so he had to be open to accepting Gloria's tricks as helpful and not wanting to hurt his feelings."

"Mm-hmm."

"So, what can we learn? What do you think the author, Peggy Rathmann, wants us to know about friendship?"

Clara thinks. "To be patient with our friends because they may be trying to help us."

When readers understand what they read, they can retell what happened, and can think beyond the text to create meaning that is not directly stated in the story, like Clara did in this example. This involves reasoning, or thinking deeply about what a text means and the effect it has on their perceptions and ideas. The acts of conversation and discussion are foundational to developing reasoning. To think, we have to respond to something written, read, or spoken.

Put another way, we reason by way of our prior experiences and thinking about our future experiences.[1] In school, when students can really comprehend and think about text, there are rich discussions. And the quality of student talk in a classroom is connected to how well students are able to problem solve, understand, and learn.[2] Finally, talking about a text can increase children's comprehension, critical thinking, and reasoning, as well as children's ability to create and defend ideas.[3]

All that to say that the conversations we're hoping to create through Active Reading are those that, first, help our children understand and then push them to learn through discussion. Asking questions is how we get that discussion started.

WHY DO WE ASK QUESTIONS?

Good readers, meaning readers who understand what they read, ask questions. Pay attention to the questions you ask as you pick up a newspaper article. For example, seeing the headline: "Mystery in a Small Town: A Quiet Couple Shot Dead, Their Daughter Missing,"[4] you may have questions that inspire you to start reading: What small town? What happened to cause the murder? Who was involved?

As you read about James and Denise Closs who were killed in their home in Barron, Wisconsin, and their thirteen-year-old daughter, Jayme, who is missing, questions propel you forward through the article: What was the Closs family like? What is Jayme like? How is the town dealing with this? What are the investigators doing to find Jayme and solve this murder mystery?

Questions move us through fiction as well. Consider picking up the classic short story "The Lottery" by Shirley Jackson.[5] In "The Lottery," the villagers in a town gather for the annual lottery. The townspeople gather stones as they prepare to each pull a slip of paper. Tessie Hutchinson joins her husband and children in the crowd. Each family draws slips of paper and it becomes clear that Tessie has the paper with the black dot on it. As Tessie argues that the process is not fair, the town encircles her and starts pelting her with stones.

At the start of the story, you'll have questions that relate to pretty much any story: Who are the characters? What is the setting? What are the people doing? What's happening?

As the story progresses, you'll ask more specific questions: What type of lottery are the people gathering for? What might they win? What's going to happen to Tess Hutchinson? Why are the children gathering stones? Why isn't anybody stepping out to stop it?

And after you finish reading, questions may linger that prompt you to think deeper about the story. Thinking about "The Lottery": What does Jackson want the reader to learn from the story about a lottery that selects a community member to be stoned? What could we learn from this story? Or is the lesson reserved for the 1940s, when the story was written?

Questions drive us forward, giving us a reason to keep reading and stoking motivation to find out what happens next. As children learn to engage with text, teaching them how to ask questions shows them how to constantly think about text, connecting what they know to what they are reading.

ASKING QUESTIONS ABOUT STORIES

Stories have an overarching structure or organization called *story grammar*. The details of stories, specific characters, settings, and problems differ from story to story, but there are overarching elements that help readers understand stories. The primary aspects of story grammar are the setting, characters, plot events, problem, resolution, and theme (Table 4.1). Depending on the length of the book, there may also be subplots, minor characters, and minor themes.

As children develop their reading skill, the stories and story grammar they engage with will become increasingly complex.

For example, reading the picture book *Make Way for Ducklings* by Robert McCloskey, a simple, classic story about ducks trying to find a home in Boston, the characters are the duck family, Michael the policeman, and the other helpers along the duck's route. The setting is Boston as a city, but specifically the Boston Public Garden. The problem is fairly simple: the ducks need a home to hatch and then raise their ducklings and they go about trying out different places before finding a good home. This book is a favorite with young readers (prekindergarten through first grade) because it is so simple and concrete; it's easy for children to follow the story.

In the illustrated chapter book series *Mercy Watson* by Kate DiCamillo, Mercy, the Watsons' pet pig, likes buttered toast and gets into unintended predicaments as she constantly tries to get more buttered toast. Her adventures involve a straightforward problem and solution and the characters act in predictable ways. The next-door neighbor, Baby Lincoln, always supports Mercy, while Eugenia, Baby's sister, thinks Mercy should not be living with the Watsons. And the stories end with the members of the community seated around plates of hot buttered toast. There is a slight advancement in the plot with more characters involved, changes in the setting, and slight variations in the plot from book to book, but these stories follow a familiar plotline and are also easy for children to follow.

As children advance to more complex chapter books, they will find more complicated plots with multiple events. For example, in the book *Sounder* by William H. Armstrong, an African American boy and his family often go hungry. Each night, the boy's father and their dog, Sounder, go out for food, but rarely find enough. The food that does appear one day is quickly followed by the sheriff and more hard times that Sounder helps the family survive. The story may be simple enough, but the events are more complex and there are various motivations and feelings to consider, including the boy's, his father's, and Sounder's.

In another example, Roald Dahl's *Charlie and the Chocolate Factory*, readers must understand and follow both what is happening to the main character (Charlie) and the minor characters (Veruca Salt, Augustus Gloop, Violet Beauregarde, and Mike Teavee). Following more than a simple plot with a core cast of characters takes working memory and the ability to focus and pay attention as the story unfolds.

When children know about story grammar, they have the schema, or background knowledge, to support comprehension of what they read.[6] *Schema* is information that we use to understand new knowledge and generate inferences.[7] Schemas are built through experience and are constantly changing. So

Table 4.1. Elements of Story Grammar

Element of Story Grammar	Description	Example: Charlotte's Web by E. B. White
Setting	The time and place that a story takes place.	On a farm in a nonspecific time
Characters	The animals, people, or other beings that are in the story. A story may have major and minor characters.	Wilbur the pig Charlotte the spider Templeton the rat The humans: Fern, Mr. and Mrs. Zuckerman
Plot events	What happens in the story. Plot events often revolve around what the character wants or a problem that they have to solve. A story may have a few main plot events, or there may be many plot events.	Wilbur is born and saved by Fern. He moves to the Zuckermans' farm and meets Charlotte. Charlotte spins the webs with writing in it.
Problem and Solution	Often the plot events revolve around a problem that the main character (or another character) has and the ways the characters try to solve that problem.	Wilbur does not want to be killed to become meat. Charlotte tries to solve this problem for Wilbur with the writing in her webs.
Theme	What the story is about or the message that we can take away from the story.	Friendship Selflessness

every time you read a story with your child, they are building their schema of what a story is. At first, their schema may include the basics (character, plot, setting), but as you read it will expand to include stories that are told through poetry, and stories that are sequenced in an unconventional order, such as starting with the end and circling back to the beginning. They'll build knowledge of subplots, minor characters, and themes.

Everything your child learns about how stories work (their schema of how stories work) will help them recall information and build new understandings.[8] When children have a deep, fully formed schema around story grammar, it helps them organize what they are reading,[9] make predictions based on what they have already read in the story,[10] generate inferences or draw conclusions about what is not explicitly written in the text,[11] and create images in their mind that help them understand the story.[12] In short, having a good understanding of how stories work provides children with the knowledge they need to really understand and enjoy stories for immediate entertainment and the deeper meaning they often convey.[13]

Active Reading teaches children about story grammar through exposure and conversation about what they read. With each picture book and novel that they are read, children learn more about story grammar. In particular, reading aloud with children as they grow older builds on children's knowledge of story grammar, extending and expanding their understanding of how stories work. Engaging elementary school–aged children in discussion of story grammar helps them deepen their understanding of how stories work and builds a foundation for complex story grammar that will help them understand what they read as they read more complex novels, even into middle and high school.[14]

The reading that children do at home also spills into school. In the classroom setting, children who were read to using Active Reading techniques (also called *dialogic reading* or *interactive shared reading*), including asking and answering questions and engaging in conversation about what they read, included more story grammar in their own stories after only eight weeks of Active Reading.[15] We help children build story grammar by asking story questions and talking about the characters, setting, plot events, and how it all fits together when we read.

Story Questions

To help children understand story grammar, we ask story questions, or questions about the characters, setting, and plot (what's happening and how it's affecting the characters). These are essentially questions that start with *who*, *what*, *when*, *why*, and *how*. They may have a clear answer from the story (e.g., what did the character do?) or they may have an answer that leaves for more interpretation (e.g., what do you think will happen next?). Asking story questions while reading helps your child articulate what they're thinking as they read, identify any things that they are not understanding, and identify important events and details. In Active Reading, these are important discussion points, but in independent reading, they're things that we want our children to do as Active Readers on their own.

Some common story questions you can ask:

- What happened to the character?
  - Why did that happen? Why do you think the character did that?
- What happened in that chapter?
  - What did you think about that chapter?
- Where is the character now?
- Who did the character meet?
- What do you think will happen next?

The questions you ask at the beginning of a story will differ from the questions that are important at the end. At the start of a story, questions about the characters, setting, and initial plot events are important. As a story unfolds, ask questions about what happens to the characters, questions about new characters that are introduced, and problems that arise. Talk about how the characters are interacting and changing. And at the end of a story, talk about how the problem was resolved, or how the plot events were resolved. After you've read, talk about what we can learn from the story as well as your child's opinions and feelings about the story (Table 4.2).[16]

For example, *Islandborn* by Junot Díaz is a picture book about a young girl, Lola. Lola's family is from "the island," but she's never been there. Everyone else in her school has a clear picture of where their family is from, but not Lola. When her teacher asks the class to draw a picture of where they are from, their family's original country, Lola has to learn about the island by asking her family for their memories.

Reading this book, in the first few pages of the story, you could ask:

- What do we learn about Lola at the start of the story? (*She's from the island, but she doesn't know much about the island because she left when she was little.*)
- What is Lola asked to do? (*To create a picture of where she's from.*)
- What is the problem? (*Lola can't remember anything; she doesn't know what to include.*)
- How is Lola feeling at the beginning of the story? (*She's feeling nervous and uncertain because she's not sure what she's going to draw and sad because everyone else knows about where they came from but she doesn't.*)

In the middle of the story, as you learn more about the problem and how Lola is trying to solve it, you may ask:

- Who does Lola talk to? What does she learn from each person? (*She talks to her cousin who tells her about the bats. She talks to Mrs. Bernard who talks about the music on the island. She talks to her brother who remembers the mangoes. She talks to her grandma about the beaches and dolphins. And she talks to others.*)
- What does Mr. Mir tell Lola? (*He tells her about the Monster.*)
- What do you think the Monster could be? (*A bad leader.*)

And at the end of the story, as Lola brings together what she's learned from her family members to generate her own understanding of "the island" and where she's from, you can ask:

- What happened when Lola showed her friends her picture? (*All the information she'd gotten about the island burst out.*)
- How did Lola feel at the end of the story? (*She felt proud of the island.*)
- What has Lola learned about the island? (*She learned that there were brave people, and that it was colorful and vibrant.*)
- What do you think the author wants us to take away? (*That we can be from somewhere and have the culture in us even if we do not live there.*)

Asking questions at the start, middle, and end of the story helps your child think about how the story is advancing and changing. These questions provide a way for you to know whether your child is understanding, and how they are building their own knowledge about the book.

Table 4.2. Asking Questions throughout a Story

	What to Talk About	*Example Questions*
Beginning	Setting Characters Initial plot events Any problems that emerge	• Where does this story take place? • Who is in the story? • What happens at the beginning? • What problems is the character having?
Middle	How the characters are changing New characters New plot events: the problem, how they are responding to it	• What happened to the character? • What do you think the character will do next? • What did we learn about this character? • How would you describe this character? • What happened? What are they doing to solve the problem?
End	How the problem was resolved The theme or lessons How the your child felt about the ending of the story	• What happened at the end? • How did the problem get resolved? • What do you think of that resolution or ending? • What do you think the author wanted us to remember?

USING QUESTIONS TO HELP CHILDREN UNDERSTAND DIFFICULT TEXTS

When you read aloud with your child, you will likely be reading books that they cannot read on their own, and may be reading books that they need help to understand. That's great—books that are really interesting and that address complex topics are ideal for Active Reading. You may find yourself having to scaffold, or support, your child's understanding of those texts, however. You can do that through the questions you ask.

When you're helping your child understand text that is complex for them, that is slightly above where they are reading on their own, there are four general questions that you can ask with any text to help your child deepen their understanding:

1. What does the text say?
2. How does the text work?
3. What does the text mean?
4. What does the text inspire you to do?[17]

1. What Does the Text Say?

Sophie and her aunt are reading Carmela Full of Wishes *by Matt de la Peña, a picture book about a little girl who has to make a wish on her birthday, but has trouble figuring out just what to wish for. As they read, Sophie's aunt asks her questions about the story: What does Carmela want for her birthday? (To go with her brother on his errands.) Where are they going? (To the laundromat, to the locksmith, to the flower shop.) What is she thinking about? (All the things she could wish for, a candy machine, a fancy hotel for her mom, her dad coming home.) These are all questions that are right there in the text.*

Asking, "What does the text say?" requires your child to understand what is written on the page. For children to understand a text at deeper levels, they have to understand the basic meaning.[18] Consider literal questions, like:

- Who is telling the story?
- How are the narrator and character connected?
- What is the setting?

All these questions get at whether your child understands what's on the page and is ready to have a deeper conversation about it. If your child easily answers literal questions, then they are ready to analyze and connect. If not, it may take slowing down, reading and talking about shorter sections of text to help your child build their knowledge of the story.

2. How Does the Text Work?

Reading Carmela Full of Wishes, *Sophie and her aunt talk about why Matt de la Peña includes Carmela's bracelets throughout the story. They talk about how the author shows what Carmela is thinking when she falls and her dandelion breaks apart. And they talk about the glare that Carmela and her brother exchange and what it shows about the two characters. Sophie's aunt asks questions that elicit conversations about how the story works: Why do you think Carmela stops jingling her bracelets at the end? (At first, we learn they are her birthday present and that they annoy her brother. But when Carmela's feelings about her brother change she takes them off so they don't bother him anymore.) How is Carmela feeling when she falls? How does the author show that? (She feels really upset. We see her think, "Don't cry!") Why do you think Carmela and her brother are glaring at each other? What does that make you think about them? (They are a typical brother and sister.)*

Questions about how the text works are about how stories work. These are questions about genre (the type of story), narration, literary devices, and vocabulary (more in Chapter 5). All these questions ask about choices the author makes and help your child think about how the author's choices influenced what ended up on the page. Questions may include:

- How does the author describe this character?
- Why do you think the author used those words?
- Where does this book take place? Why do you think the author chose this setting?

Asking a few questions about text structure and how the text is organized can open a conversation about how the text was created, even if you're just noticing and wondering about it.

3. What Does the Text Mean?

After they read, Sophie's aunt asks her about what the story could mean to her. What do you think Carmela wished for? What do you think Carmela's brother thinks of Carmela? How do you know?

Asking about the meaning of text asks children to think about a deeper meaning in the text with questions like:

- What does that author think of ___?
- How do you know?
- What does the character think of ___? How do you know?

As children think about and talk about what the text means, they develop opinions and arguments. This is where most of the conversation may occur as your child's thoughts and ideas will have to be shaped through your conversation. Asking, "How do you know?" encourages your child to give examples from the text. If your child can't cite evidence right away, you can provide your own ideas as well.

4. What Does the Text Inspire You to Do?

Reading Carmela Full of Wishes, *Sophie's aunt asks, What does this book make you wonder about? How does Carmela's brother treat her? How does he show her he cares about her? Can you think a way you could do that too?*

Once your child has had an experience with a text, they may want to write about it, act it out, read another book by the same author, or take another action. These questions include:

- What would you tell the author?
- Who could you share this book with?
- Who might enjoy this book?

This brings the conversation you've had into the real world for children. You may only ask these types of questions after you've finished reading a book together, and that's okay.

THINKING CRITICALLY ABOUT STORIES

Having a basic understanding of a text is an important start, but we want our children to be able to analyze and think critically about what they read. Critical thinking means thinking more deeply about a topic. When we go beyond memorizing facts or retelling a story, we're engaging in critical thinking. In our adult lives, this may occur when we research a topic and incorporate information from different articles and books to form our opinion, then argue for that opinion in conversation, or when we read multiple books by the same author and explain why we like that particular author.

When children engage in critical thinking, they're taking what they know from a story, making inferences, connecting them to other ideas, re-creating them in new ways, and applying them to new problems. In Active Reading, this happens through discussion and connection (more in Chapters 6 and 7). When we encourage children to take what we read about together and play with the ideas, we're encouraging critical thinking.

How Do Children Develop Critical Thinking?

Critical thinking occurs when we use our knowledge to compare and contrast, explain, evaluate ideas and form opinions, understand other perspectives, think about solutions, and predict what might happen in the future. These are skills that extend far beyond Active Reading, but we can encourage children to start thinking critically using books that lend themselves to conversations about how characters are the same and different, or how to solve a problem, or how to use information we already learned by reading to predict what may happen next in the story.

Critical thinking is primarily a language skill, which makes Active Reading a great way to develop critical thinking as children are encouraged to explain themselves and learn the language of critical thinking, such as "if . . . then" and "because." As children's language grows, they'll be able to do more critical thinking as well.

Two key critical thinking skills that come through in asking questions are inferencing and making predictions.

1. Inferencing involves taking what they know about a situation or character and what is stated in the text to draw their own, reasonable conclusion.
2. Making predictions involves taking what they know about what they've already read and anticipating what could come next.

Both inferencing and making predictions make reading more meaningful, and draw the reader into what they're engaged with. Children can start thinking critically from a young age, and asking questions is a good way to start.

How to Raise a Critical Thinker

Building critical thinking skills in our children requires asking questions, but it also requires giving your child time to think about a response, and following up with more questions to extend their thinking. Responding to your child's questions with wonders and encouragement to seek additional information will push the conversation toward higher-order thinking.

At the end of the first chapter of Ramona Quimby, Age 8 *by Beverly Cleary, Evan, eight, and his mother talk about the story.*

"What do you think of Ramona so far?" his mom asks.

"I think she's funny."

"I wonder if the book will get even funnier. She was really into her eraser. Why do you think it was so important to her?"

"Because it was new."

"Yes, and who gave it to her?"

"Her dad."

"Yes, for the first day of school. I think that may have made it important to her, that her dad gave it to her."

"Yeah."

"So what do you think is important to Ramona right now?"

"Her family and her eraser."

"I agree, and making her parents happy seems really important to her."

As you read with your child, be aware of how you respond. While you should provide encouragement, especially when they answer correctly or you think they have a really insightful idea, you don't have to respond with praise or feedback to every answer. Providing open-ended responses and asking more questions can take the conversation in new directions, as Evan and his mom found in this exchange.

Responding in an open-ended way, and with more questions about what you're reading, also encourages the conversation that we want to gain during Active Reading. As mentioned earlier, conversation, or discussion, is an important component of comprehension that children learn through.[19] Through the conversation you have about stories, Active Reading gives you a chance to show children how you make meaning of what you read, and then pass that along to your child as they practice the same thinking.[20]

As in the previous example, your role in the conversation, in addition to helping start it through questions, is to continue it. You can do this by expanding and eliciting:[21]

- Expand: When your child answers a question, restate what they said and add additional information.
- Elicit: Ask them to give additional information and have a conversation with you by asking additional questions.

The purpose is not to have what feels like a verbal tennis game; the point is to have an authentic conversation. Talk about answers that are interesting to you. If you ask a question and are surprised by your child's answer, ask a question, like: What makes you think that? If you have an idea about the story, throw that out there and ask your child what they think. Look for disagreement and ask your child to explain their point of view, defending their opinion with examples from the book.

GET KIDS TO ASK QUESTIONS

As Evan and his mom continue to read Ramona Quimby, Age 8, *Evan starts asking questions. "Why does Ramona want to be horrid to Willa Jean?" "Why does Ramona want hard-boiled eggs for lunch?" "Why did Ramona want to smash an egg on her head?"*

Some of the questions are, to be honest, unanswerable (Why does Ramona want hard-boiled eggs for lunch?), but the process and practice of asking ques-

More ways to answer questions that encourage critical thinking:

- Encourage your child to find an answer from another source (and get them to read more!)
  - Where could we look to find the answer?
- Encourage alternate explanations or brainstorm ideas:
  - What do you think? What are some ideas that could explain that?
- Encourage your child to seek out additional information to satisfy their curiosity:
  - If your child has a question that nags at them and they want to explore it, encourage them!

tions shows that Evan is understanding and thinking about the story. That's the ultimate goal—that our children are asking the questions as they read.

During Active Reading, especially if Active Reading is new for you and your child, you'll likely ask most of the questions. After all, you have decades of experience asking questions while your child is still learning. But, over time, you want your child to ask questions both while you're reading together and on their own.

To encourage your child to ask questions:

- Slow down. Pause between sections or chapters in the story. Leave space for them to insert a question or wonder.
- Ask: What are you wondering? Or: What questions do you have?
- When you read picture books, leave time to talk about the pictures.
- When reading chapter books, ask about what your child is wondering after each chapter.

TELL ME MORE

In Active Reading, asking questions engages children by inviting them into a conversation. We use questions to ensure that our children understand what the text says, and to help them think through how to make inferences, form opinions, and express ideas about a text and teach them how to use questions to understand what they read on their own. In the next chapter, we build from asking questions to talking about new words we find in books.

* * *

WHAT TO REMEMBER

- The goal of Active Reading is to have conversations about what we read. Questions help those conversations become about more than what happened in the story or what we learned on each page.
- Questions help move us through stories and get knowledge from nonfiction text. As children learn to read, asking questions teaches children how to constantly think about what they are reading, connecting known to new information.
- Active Reading allows us to expose children to more complex story grammar, or how stories are organized, than they can read on their own, deepening their understanding of story elements and how stories work. When children have their own understanding of story grammar, they are better able to organize and understand stories they read on their own.
- Story questions—questions about the characters, setting, plot, and other core story elements—help highlight what is interesting and unique about the beginning, middle, and end of a story.
  - At the beginning of a story, talk about the characters, setting, and initial problem.
  - In the middle of a story, talk about how the problem is changing and developing, how the characters are responding to the problem, and what they are doing.
  - At the end of the story, ask about how the problem was solved, and what your child thinks about the story.
- Four general questions you can ask while you read include:
  - What does the text say?
  - How does the text work?
  - What does the text mean?
  - What does the text inspire you to do?
- Build your child's critical thinking skills by asking questions that encourage them to make inferences and provide open-ended answers, and responding to their discussion skills by expanding on what they say and eliciting new information.

5

Build Vocabulary

Reading *Dory Fantasmagory: The Real True Friend* by Abby Hanlon to my kindergarten-aged daughter, we come across words that she isn't familiar with: *outfit, self-portrait, nostrils, gagging*.

At each word that is new to her, we stop and talk about them.

"What does outfit mean?" she asks.

"It's the clothes you wear. Like, Dory is getting her back-to-school outfit, so she's choosing the clothes she'll wear on the first day of school."

"Oh."

"The clothes you wore today were your outfit. And, for you, in kindergarten, you wear a uniform so you kind of wear the same outfit each day."

Active Reading is a way that I've built my own kids' vocabulary, and helped them find even more words they don't know in books. Think about the reading you've done with your child already:

- What words have you come across and talked about?
- What words has your child learned from a story and used in their everyday conversation?

Reading the first chapter of Ramona Quimby, Age 8 *by Beverly Cleary, Evan and his mom stop to talk about the word* accuracy.

"Accuracy means when you get something all right, with no mistakes," says his mom.

"Oh."

"Ramona wanted everyone to be accurate, but she stopped demanding ac-curacy, meaning that she stopped making other people be right all the time. Can you think of a time when you wanted something to be accurate?"

"My homework?" Evan suggested.

"Oh, yeah, when you wanted your math homework to be all correct, yes that's accuracy."

Before reading *Ramona Quimby*, Evan's mom may never have used the word accuracy with him and she may never have thought to teach him that word. But when the word comes up in the story, as one of the first things that we learn about how Ramona is changing as she heads into third grade, it's the perfect opportunity to build his vocabulary.

The *B* in the ABCs of Active Reading is *Build vocabulary*. In fact, when it comes to reading aloud, building your child's vocabulary may be the most important thing that you can do. Reading aloud to your child helps build vocabulary by providing lots of words. Then your child will use the words they learn to better read and understand on their own.

The trick to build your child's vocabulary is, first, choosing words to talk about and, then, talking about them in a way that your child understands what the words mean and how to use them. Ultimately, we want those words to be in our children's everyday vocabulary. In this chapter, we talk about the importance of vocabulary as children grow as readers, and how to choose and teach words through Active Reading.

VOCABULARY IS IMPORTANT, IMPERATIVE, AND SIGNIFICANT

The need for a rich vocabulary goes beyond reading. Vocabulary is an important part of communicating—the richer our vocabularies, the better we can tell a story; recall an experience; describe a process; and articulate our feelings, hopes, and dreams; not to mention understand what others are telling us. As a parent, you've probably already watched as your child's vocabulary grew from a few commands or demands (no! bottle) to complex sentences and the ability to intricately describe an altercation with a sibling or friend.

Even at a young age, vocabulary is an important indicator for kids' future success. For example, your child's vocabulary in first grade is predictive of their high school reading achievement.[1] And children use their vocabularies every day: a third grader will read as many as one million words of text across the year.[2] They'll read another million words in fourth grade, fifth grade, and so on. That's a lot of words.

To be sure, many of those words are common (*party, summer, look, game*), some of the words are less common (*giddy, ecstatic*), and some are specifically related to one topic (*crustacean*, *hurricane*). But the more your child reads and the more they read books that are increasingly difficult and about topics that are new to them, the more they'll encounter interesting and complex vocabulary. So, with the sheer number of words that children need to read, it's probably no surprise that vocabulary is related to reading ability and school achievement.[3]

The number of words a child knows is also important because it helps them understand what they read; a child's reading comprehension and vocabulary are strongly correlated, meaning that the more words a child knows, the better their reading comprehension.[4] As your child reads on their own, they will inevitably encounter words that they don't know. Once they've sounded those words out, they'll rely on their vocabulary to recognize and understand the words within sentences, paragraphs, and stories.[5]

So vocabulary is a high-stakes skill and one of the most important things that you can build in your children that will set them on the path to success. But how do children learn new words? You may remember learning vocabulary through lists of words that you had to look up in the dictionary or memorize definitions. If you do, it's probably not a surprise to you that this is not the best way to learn new words. For word learning to stick with kids, we need to teach vocabulary through conversation that encourages kids to use each new word.

How Children Learn Words

As children grow, they first learn words that are in their environment, spoken by their parents, shouted at them by siblings, and cooed to them by grandparents. Interacting with a parent in the kitchen, a child may learn *spoon* and *more*. Playing house with an adult or older child, a toddler may learn the words *pot*, *bake*, and *spatula*. They also learn words through everyday experiences (learning *nocturnal*, *bamboo*, and *hibernate* after a trip to the zoo). And they learn words through books and being read to.

As children get older, reading becomes increasingly important as a way to learn new words. When that shift happens, learning words without instruction becomes harder. Put another way, learning lots of words through reading is hard to do without help.[6] It's estimated that of one thousand unfamiliar words that we read, we'll learn between five and fifteen of those words simply by reading.[7] So, just reading builds some vocabulary, but kids still need to talk about words to learn as many words as they can through reading. And to learn words from reading, children must be taught the correct definition and then exposed to the words over and over. They need lots of experience with words that they hear and learn from conversation and books.

In reading, they also need to learn how to infer word meaning from context.[8] For example, in *Matilda* by Roald Dahl, a child will have to infer that the word *twaddle* (which is a word not often used in American English) means someone who is foolish or silly. They will make that inference using the previous information that how parents feel about their children is often inaccurate and silly.

The good news: a child's vocabulary grows quickly and the more words they learn, the easier it is to add new words to their vocabulary. When children have a large vocabulary, they can learn new words faster because they have existing knowledge to connect those new words to.[9] Active Reading is a way to expose your child to new words and build their vocabulary.

FINDING WORDS: THE POWER OF BOOKS

Recall that your child will be reading as many as one million words a year by the time they're in third grade.[10] Not all those words will be new words, and not all of them will even be words worth teaching them. Of the about fifteen thousand word families that make up those one million words, eight thousand will be familiar words that they use in everyday conversation and have seen in books that they read, even the "easy" ones that they may quickly grow out of. There are also words that fit into word "families" with a core root word that is changed with prefix and suffix combinations (e.g., the word *appear* is the root word that helps create other words like *disappear, reappear, appearance*, and others). These are what researchers call *Tier 1* or familiar words.[11] They're not words that need to be taught during Active Reading. The kinds of words you'll think about teaching are rare words, academic words, and phrases (Table 5.1).

Rare Words

Of the fifteen thousand word families that children need to know, about seven thousand are Tier 2 or "rare" words. These are words that are not used as much when we talk to our children or even when we talk to other adults, but are used in text. Rare words are words that are common, but not used often. Think of synonyms for common words, like *depressed* or *blue* for *sad*. They are also used across genres and topics, and you'll encounter them in books from novels to science articles. For example, you may see the word *pleasant* in fiction (it's used in the novel *Stuart Little* by E. B. White to describe Stuart) and in nonfiction (it may be used to describe the weather on a summer's day).

Table 5.1. Common, Rare, and Academic Words in Books

Book Title and Author	Common Words	Rare Words	Academic Words
From Caterpillar to Butterfly by Deborah Heiligman	Grow Eat School Bigger	Damp Crumpled	Hatched Molting Chrysalis Proboscis
A Seed Is Sleepy by Dianna Aston	Sleepy Seed Sunlight Water	Reveal Blooms Dash Adventurous Dormant	Flowering Gymnosperms Orchid Roots Pod Monocot Germinate
Miss Rumphius by Barbara Cooney	Ship Beautiful Seed	Bother Scattered Flung Hollows	Wharves Conservatory Lupine
Dancing in the Wings by Debbie Allen	Jump Spin Faster Dance	Talent Festival Imitate Potential	Tendu Duet Backstage Audition Adagio

For younger children, picture books are an important way that children are exposed to and learn new vocabulary.[12] High-quality picture books (see Appendix A for recommendations) are wonderful for discovering rare words.[13] For example, the book *Officer Buckle and Gloria* by Peggy Rathmann has the following rare words: *command, announce, discovered, audience, enormous,* and *shocked*. Novels are another rich source of rare words. In the novel *Stuart Little* by E. B. White, rare words appear frequently in the first few pages: *shinny, unusual, preferred, delighted, unsuitable, solemnly, agreeable, horrified, inquired*.

Academic Words

Academic words are tied to a specific context or topic. Readers need to understand these words to read about the topic. In the nonfiction book *A Seed Is Sleepy*, by Dianna Aston, words like *germinate, cone, cotyledon* (seed leaves), and *gymnosperms* (seeds that don't have fruit around them) are all vocabulary specific to seeds. The book *See inside Your Body*, by Katie Daynes, uses words that are used when talking about body systems: *organ, cells, nerve, blood, bone*. In both cases, talking about seeds and body systems,

In the book *Strega Nona* by Tomie dePaola, there lots of rare words: *cure, potions, fetch, confess, applause, compliments, barricade*. In *Pinduli* by Janell Cannon the rare words include *spied, exquisite, soggy, unpleasant, vanished, pallid, atrocious, quavered, wrath, tormenters, authority*.

Pull a few picture books off of your shelves at home or at the local library. Flip through the pages.

- What rare words jump out at you?
- Now that you're looking for them, are there more rare words than you thought there would be?

the academic vocabulary words will generally be used to refer to that topic. These words are important for background knowledge (more in Chapter 7).

Often, academic words are easier for children to learn because of their inherent interest in a topic. Also, academic words are often defined within books that we read to children and in books for young children with a picture or text, so they will have help defining the word as they read. For example, *The Magic School Bus* books contain lots of text features that help children define words, like the explanations of words on the side of each page and captions that accompany each picture.

Understanding Phrases

As children read more and more complex books, they'll also have to understand how words work together in phrases or in figurative language, like idioms, metaphors, and analogies. For example, in the picture book *Officer Buckle and Gloria* by Peggy Rathmann, children must understand the phrase "sit at attention" (when a dog sits up and shows that it is ready), "eyes popped" (when the students showed surprised), and "stick with your buddy" (to stay with something). All of those phrases are made up of words that your child likely knows, but put together and in the context of the book, they have a slightly different meaning than the words have on their own.

Readers often use inferences to understand phrases and figurative language (more on inferences in Chapter 6). For example, in the picture book *Last Stop on Market Street* by Matt de la Peña, air "smelled like freedom," "a bus breathes fire," and "rhythm lifted" the character out of the bus. All of those phrases require some inference to understand. As you read aloud, pulling out figurative language like analogies "smelled like freedom," personification "the bus breathes fire," and others (Table 5.2) will teach your child that phrases can convey meaning, and how to understand new phrases as they read.

Table 5.2.   Figurative Language

Type of Figurative Language	Definition	Example
Alliteration	When the first words in a phrase or sentence have the same sound	Annie's aunt ate eight alligators.
Metaphor	Comparison between two things	The wind is a dragon. Mom is a tornado when she's angry.
Simile	Comparison of two things that uses the word *like* or *as*	The pond is as still as glass. Her legs are as long as stilts.
Onomatopoeia	A word that makes a sound	Splat Crash Bang Ding dong
Personification	When the author gives something that is not a human the characteristics of a person	The wind danced and whistled.
Idiom	A phrase that has a real meaning that is different than its literal meaning	That's the way the cookie crumbles. Keep an eye out for her. You're pulling my leg.
Hyperbole	An extreme exaggeration	She makes the worst chili in the world.

CHOOSING WORDS DURING ACTIVE READING

We know that it's important to teach the words we find in books.[14] And it's not enough to read the books to our children and expect them to learn the vocabulary; we have to explain and talk about the words. That's where Active Reading comes in; children who are engaged in Active Reading techniques learned more words compared with children who were read the same stories without Active Reading.[15]

In picture books, rare words may jump out at you and, with the short length of the book, you can stop and talk about them easily without stopping the story too much. But when you're reading chapter books or novels, there may be a lot of rare words, or you may not know when to stop and talk about a word without losing the flow of the story. In novels, look for rare words that are important for understanding the story. These are recurring words, words that describe important characters or events, and words that you think your child will get "hung up on" if they don't understand; they are all worth stopping and talking about.

For example, the book *Matilda* by Roald Dahl has many words you could focus on (there may be more words than usual because Dahl is a British

writer, so his way of phrasing isn't familiar to American readers at times).
In the first pages, Dahl lays out the idea that parents are so blinded by their
love for their children that they think their children are only wonderful and
don't see their children's weaknesses (which he later contrasts with Matilda's
parents, who don't see her gifts). In these pages, stop to talk about the phrases
that will help your child understand the big idea that Dahl is laying out, which
is part of the humor of the book. Words and phrases including "qualities of a
genius," "revolting," and "doting" are important for understanding the gist of
what Dahl is trying to say.

When your child chooses their own book to read, you may have heard of
the five-finger rule. That's the idea that if they read to the end of a page and
have read five words that they don't know, then the book is too difficult.
With reading aloud, there isn't any specific number of new words that are too
many, but if your child can't retell what just happened in the story or you find
yourself stopping to talk about new words so often that you lose the story, it's
probably time to put that book down and choose another.

BUILDING YOUR CHILD'S VOCABULARY
THROUGH ACTIVE READING

Talking about words in context in picture books or in read-alouds is the most
effective way for children to build their vocabulary.[16] Children learn words by
using them in conversation, writing, and reading. This gets children thinking
about what words mean and how they connect to the story, to their lives, and
to other words.

To teach your child new words while reading with them:

1. Give a child-friendly definition.
2. Connect the word to the story; ask a question about how the word is
   used in the story.
3. Connect the word to the child's life; talk about how you've used or seen
   that word in other stories and in life.
4. Use the word outside of reading!

For example, using the book *Stuart Little* by E. B. White, Stuart had the
"shy manner of a mouse." You might pull out the phrase "shy manner," specifically the word *manner*.

First, provide a child-friendly definition.

"A manner is a way of acting, so Stuart was shy. He always acted shy."

Then connect the word to the story by asking questions about how the word is used in the story.

"What did Stuart do that was shy?"

Next, connect the word to your child's life by talking about how you've used or seen that word in other situations. You could talk about other people you know who have shy manners or ask your child to think about another character they've seen in books or movies who is shy. And as you continue to read, talk about how Stuart demonstrates his shy manner throughout the story.

Talking about words in this way, providing enough information so that children know what the words mean and have experience using the word in multiple contexts, gives them the knowledge and practice to incorporate the words into their vocabulary.

BECOMING WORD LEARNERS: DEVELOPING WORD CONSCIOUSNESS

Angie Allison, mom of three, makes reading a regular part of the daily routine. Her youngest, Scarlett, who is in third grade, notices when her parents are reading and grabs her own book to join in. Allison notices that when they are reading together, and when Scarlett, who loves everything from *Fancy Nancy* books to *The Lemonade War* series, reads on her own, she asks the meanings of words she doesn't know. That's word consciousness; Scarlett recognizes when she doesn't know a word and will stop to figure it out before diving back into the book.

Eventually, as you start talking about the words you find in books, your child will, like Scarlett, start asking what words mean. When your child starts interrupting you to ask about new words, that's great! It means that they're developing word consciousness, or an awareness of and interest in words.[17] This word consciousness can lead to even more vocabulary learning.[18]

The goal of word consciousness is that children will consistently seek to understand what words mean and develop curiosity about language.[19] When children are curious about how words work and what words mean, they're likely to build their own vocabulary by seeking out new words on their own. While word consciousness is not something that you can teach directly, you can cultivate it. Active Reading will develop your child's word consciousness as you pull out words and talk about them. There are other ways to make your child into a voracious word learner:

- Encourage playing with words by brainstorming synonyms for new words, thinking of different ways to describe things you see, and challenging your child to get as specific as possible with their words.
- Research where words come from. Look words up in the dictionary and thesaurus to find out their origins, different definitions, and synonyms and antonyms.
- Model to your child that words are interesting and fun by noticing and exclaiming over new words that you learn. When adults are engaged in learning new words and are curious about where words come from, children get the idea that words are fun.[20]

Similar to Jim Trelease's argument about selling reading to our kids through reading aloud, getting interested in and showing excitement about words sells vocabulary and word learning to our kids.

WORDS, WORDS, WORDS

Your child doesn't have to develop a deep, dictionary-specific understanding of every word to become a strong reader. The more words they know, even if it's a basic knowledge of the word, the better they are when it comes to expanding their vocabulary, being aware of words, and deepening their knowledge of different words over time. Active Reading is a way to start catapulting your child's interest in words, word knowledge, and love of vocabulary. In the next chapter, we discuss the *C* in Active Reading: making Connections, starting with fiction.

* * *

WHAT TO REMEMBER

- Vocabulary is an important part of what we learn from reading, and what we need to read well. The greater a child's vocabulary, the greater their reading achievement.[21] Children do learn new words by reading, but we must also teach children the meaning of words they come across in text to help them understand and remember new words.
- We teach children rare words, or words that are more common in books than in conversation, through Active Reading. We also teach figurative language (idioms, metaphors, analogies) and phrases, which will help children understand more complex text.

- In chapter books and novels, look for rare words that are necessary for understanding the story. These could be recurring words, words that describe important characters or events, and words that you think your child will get stuck on.
- When your child has chosen their own book to read, if they cannot retell what they read, then there may be too many unknown words. That means that book is either great for you to read together (so you can help them understand the new vocabulary) or it may be a book they can put away and come back to later.
- Teaching words through Active Reading involves creating conversation around the word. To do this, you can follow the process:
  ◦ Give a child-friendly definition.
  ◦ Connect the word to the story with a question.
  ◦ Connect the word to the child's life with a question or comment.
  ◦ Use the word outside of reading.

6

Make Connections to the Child's World

Fiction

Connecting to Stories

As an elementary schooler I read and reread *The Baby-Sitters Club* books by Ann M. Martin. The stories about preteens Kristy, Mary Anne, Claudia, and Stacey fascinated me. I was just starting to become interested in babysitting and trying to navigate friendships at the age when clubs were cool. I connected to the excitement of being in charge as a young babysitter, the anticipation of starting middle school, and the ups and downs of friendships. And I know I'm not the only person who started their own babysitter's club in the 1990s.

Perhaps you have a similar story with a book that you connected with during your childhood, a book that engaged you at just the right time and that resonated with you because of the characters, plot, or emotions it brought up. Think about a story (book or movie) that you felt a strong connection to as a child (or as an adult):

- What was it about that story and that time in your life that helped you connect to it?
- How did your connection to that story help you understand it?
- How did your connection help you understand the broader world?

Matilda by Roald Dahl is the ultimate elementary school novel. The main character, Matilda, is a precocious five-year-old, characterized by her love of books, with just enough magical ability to help her beloved teacher, Ms. Honey, while outsmarting her nemesis, the Trunchbull (the school principal).

The story resonates with young children who, entering the elementary school where they seem to have the least amount of power of anyone in the school building, can connect with Matilda and her predicament, and see the humor and fun in her story.

Part of the reason *Matilda* resonates with children is because they connect with it so readily. Dahl based Matilda's school experience off of his own boarding school experience, which he found particularly awful.[1] This is not to say that all children find school awful, but that Dahl captured and exaggerated aspects of school and added his own brand of humor, wit, and excitement to make it a story that children still connect with today.

When we do Active Reading with young children (ages two to four), the *C* in the ABCs is about connecting directly to their world.[2] Connecting the experiences in books to young children's lives makes reading relevant and supports language development as they communicate their own stories and experiences. As children grow, connecting to their world is the most basic form of connection.

For children age five through nine, connecting expands to include using what children already know from their experiences and other books to make inferences and to deepen their understanding of the story. Ultimately, this builds their comprehension and increases the relevance of stories as they generalize what they read about in stories to their world.

This chapter covers how to make connections with fiction that support children's ability to connect to stories to make inferences and predictions, and to learn about the world.

MAKING INFERENCES: CONNECTING OLD AND NEW INFORMATION

Frank, who is six years old, and his dad are reading Alexander and the Terrible, Horrible, No Good, Very Bad Day *by Judith Viorst. In the story, Alexander is sitting at the breakfast table, watching his brothers get treats in their cereal boxes while Alexander's box is full of. . .cereal.*

"How do you think Alexander feels?" his dad asks.

"Probably jealous," Frank replies.

"How do you know?"

"That's how I would feel if that happened to me, like when Judy got the blue ball in her goodie bag from the party and mine was the only bag without a ball."

In this example, Frank has made a basic inference. He's taking what he knows from personal experience and applying it to his understanding of the story. Viorst never writes that Alexander feels jealous—it's left to the reader to figure that out on their own. However, if the reader cannot make that inference, they are missing an important part of the story.

As the story continues, Alexander doesn't get to sit by the window in his carpool. His friends decide they are not best friends with Alexander anymore. His mom forgot to pack dessert in his lunch. And he is the only one with a cavity at the dentist.

"How does Alexander feel now?" Frank's dad asks, after reading that the shoe store didn't have the kind of shoes Alexander wanted.

"Really frustrated," says Frank.

"What makes you think that?"

"All these things have happened to him and none of them are good."

"Yeah," his dad agrees, "he never gets what he wants."

Making inferences involves drawing a conclusion by combining what we know directly from the text with new information, from our own experience or from information given to us in the text. When reading, we use knowledge that we have gained from our experience, or from reading the story, and combine it with new information in the book to infer.[3] In the example, Frank used information that he had from previous experiences (what it means to feel jealous or frustrated) with new information (all the horrible things that happen to Alexander) to make an inference that helps him better connect with and understand the story.

As he continues reading, he can validate that conclusion using the images of Alexander scowling or his (empty) threats to move to Australia. Put another way, when we make inferences, we take information that is written in the text and build an understanding or meaning that goes beyond what is written in the words by adding our own knowledge. Sometimes we call this "reading between the lines" because we build an understanding that is not written on the page.

Inferencing helps readers fill in missing information in a text to create a complete understanding of what is happening.[4] For example, think about these sentences: *Laura picked up the gift. It was light as a feather. She shook it. There was no sound.* Simple inferences, like connecting the "gift" and "it" in the subsequent sentences are made automatically as we develop skill in reading and using language.

To understand what we read, we must make lots of inferences.[5] Indeed, we are inferring almost constantly as we read. It's concerning that even many adults who struggle with reading lack the ability to infer quickly and accurately.[6] As children learn to read, they need lots of practice making inferences so the skill becomes automatic. As you read aloud to your child, in addition to simple inferences, you will come across two primary types of inferences: cause and effect and relationship.

Cause-and-Effect Inferences

Cause-and-effect inferences are made when readers make connections between an initial event (the antecedent) and the consequence of that event.[7] For example, read the sentences: *Rain spattered on the window. A thunderclap shook the panes. I looked out the window and saw that the yard was littered with broken branches.* Using the information from the first sentences, you can infer that a rainstorm caused the damage in the yard.

In the book *Thank You, Mr. Falker* by Patricia Polacco, Trisha is a young girl who struggles to learn to read. We read about her experiences struggling to read, about how she feels different and then stupid. When she moves to a new school, she thinks it will be different, but she still has trouble reading. So when we read that Trisha wants to go to school "less and less," we can infer that Trisha doesn't want to go to school because it is difficult and because she feels frustrated with schoolwork. This cause-and-effect inference that the reader makes builds across the book as we see Trisha in the various situations.

Relationship Inferences

Relationship inferences occur when readers integrate information across multiple sentences to understand how things interact or connect.[8] For example, read the sentences: *Sarah saw the freshly baked plate of cookies on the kitchen counter. She tugged at her waistband. She sighed and reached in the fruit bowl for an apple.* Without knowing Sarah, you can connect the information across the sentences to infer that Sarah is trying to lose weight, and that she would rather eat cookies than an apple.

In another example, in the picture book *Officer Buckle and Gloria* by Peggy Rathmann, Officer Buckle gives presentations about safety tips that typically put the children in the audience to sleep. However, when Gloria the dog accompanies him, she acts out his safety tips, and the audience sits up and cheers. From that, we can infer that the children are laughing because of Gloria, not because of Officer Buckle. And after Gloria performs again and again without Officer Buckle noticing, when he eventually finds out what Gloria has been doing behind his back, we can infer that he feels very hurt. The events in the story inform what we know about Officer Buckle, Gloria, and their relationship, and help us make better inferences as we read further in the story.

HOW DO YOU KNOW? HELPING CHILDREN MAKE INFERENCES

Anjali, who is seven years old, is reading Dory Fantasmagory *by Abby Hanlon with her grandfather. Together, they read the illustrated chapter book about Dory (also known as Rascal), the youngest of three siblings who has a vivid imagination. "What do Dory's brother and sister think of her?" Anjali's grandfather asks.*

"They don't want to play with her," Anjali says.

"So, what do you think they think about her?" her grandfather nudges.

"Well, they don't like her. They think she's annoying."

"I think you're right," her grandfather says. "How do you know?"

Anjali points to a picture in the book. "Right here, her brother and sister are complaining about everything Dory is doing, and they are rolling their eyes and saying, 'Leave us alone.'"

"Yeah, that's the kind of thing someone would do if they were annoyed," her grandfather says.

We can help children learn how to make inferences by talking about how they connect what they know from their experience, the words in the book, or the pictures with what we read together.[9]

First, ask a question that encourages the child to infer information. Questions should be open ended, but still connected to the story. For example, Anjali's grandfather asked: *What do Dory's brother and sister think of her?*

If the child answers correctly, confirm their answer and encourage the child to provide more information about how they came to that conclusion by asking, "How do you know?"

Then talk about how your child made the inference. You can say:

- What in the story made you think that?
- What do you see in the picture that made you think that?
- What did you know that helped you understand that?
- That's a great conclusion. What helped you come to that idea?

You can continue the conversation by asking the child to connect whatever you are talking about to their own life. If you are talking about a character, does your child have that same trait? Or if you are talking about an experience, have they experienced something similar? Did they handle it in the same way?

Taking your child through this process helps children think through how they are connecting information that is not stated in the text with information that is in the story. It also extends the conversation and gives you information about what information your child has grasped and how they are connecting to the story.

How Do You Know?

Engage children in conversation to help them make inferences and talk through the process of making inferences.

1. Ask a question that encourages the child to make an inference. These questions often start with *why* or *how*:

   • Why did the character do that?
   • How does the character feel now?

2. If the child makes a correct inference, confirm the child's answer:

   • That's a great conclusion.

3. Then ask them to think about their inference:

   • Does the author say that?
   • How do you know?
   • What in the story made you think that?
   • What do you know that helped you understand that?

It's important to keep in mind that it will take many conversations for your child to become good at making inferences. Each time they infer, your child is pairing new information from the book with different background knowledge. As they talk with you, they are practicing the thinking skills of making inferences, which is not limited to that one inference. Focusing on the process of connecting information as you talk with them will help them think it through and see how to make inferences with lots of different types of information.

We want our children to make inferences each time they read. With each sentence, the information they have will change, and they should constantly be asking how new information adds to and changes what they already know. You can help make inferencing a habit for your child by stopping when new information comes into a story and talk about what this means. First, what is the new information? And how might it affect what you already know about the story?

As children gain independence and get better at answering inference questions, step back and ask them to do more of the thinking on their own. Ask open-ended questions like, "What happened in that story?" Then ask, "What did the author tell you in the story? What did you think about that character or story?"

MAKING PREDICTIONS

Emily and her mother are at a pivotal point in Charlie and the Chocolate Factory *by Roald Dahl. Charlie is at Willy Wonka's Chocolate Factory and they are about to enter the Chocolate Room. "What do you think will happen next?" asks Emily's mother.*

At this point in the story, given that Charlie has proven himself a sensible character, compared with the other kids who are coming to the chocolate factory, it would be incorrect for Emily to predict that Charlie is going to do something abhorrent, like steal the chocolate or get into trouble. But understanding Charlie's love of chocolate and the already unusual visit, it would be logical for her to predict that Charlie will eat lots of chocolate or find something completely unexpected.

A prediction is another type of inference, or educated guess, that is specifically about what will happen next in the story. Even as adult readers, we are constantly making predictions, and aligning those predictions with what actually happens. When something occurs in a story that does not align with what we thought could happen, it just doesn't feel right. Making predictions is a skill that helps children comprehend what they read by focusing on what they have already read and understood, and connecting it to new information in the story. This keeps them thinking about what has happened, even as they think ahead.

Teach predicting by stopping at pivotal points in the story. In picture books, this may be at the end of a scene when the setting is about to change, or when the character is about to make a change. In the picture book *Stand Tall, Molly Lou Melon* by Patty Lovell, this could be before Molly Lou starts her new school. In *Thank You, Mr. Falker* by Patricia Polacco, it's when Trisha starts fifth grade with a new teacher. When reading chapter books, the end of each chapter is a good time to think about what could happen next. (Authors often end chapters at a cliff-hanger, meaning that they end on a particularly suspenseful part, leaving the reader wondering, what *will* happen next?) If you are reading a chapter book across multiple days, talking about what has happened so far and what you think will happen in the chapter you are about to read is a good way to ease back into the story.

To help your child make a prediction, you can ask a series of questions: What happened in the story (in this chapter or on this page)? What do you think will happen next? What in the story makes you think that?

After Emily's mother asked her what she thinks will happen when Charlie enters the Chocolate Room, Emily says, "I think Charlie will go crazy trying to eat as much chocolate as he can."

"What makes you think that?" her mother asks.

"Because he never gets chocolate anytime except for his birthday, so he might get greedy."

"That's a good idea," her mother says. "He does love chocolate and he doesn't get to eat it a lot. What do you think will happen to the other characters?"

"I think one of them will get greedy and Willy Wonka will kick them out of the tour." "That's an interesting idea. Let's see what happens." They turn the page.

Perhaps the most important thing to do when making a prediction is what happens afterward.

Remember to Circle Back

After you make a prediction, come back to it after the story or chapter. Was the prediction correct? If it wasn't entirely correct, was it partially correct or not at all correct? And now that they know what happened, what information at the start of the story could have helped them see what was actually going to happen?

Emily and her mother read the next chapters. They read about Charlie being awestruck by the Chocolate Room, the Oompa Loompas, and Augustus Gloop going up the pipe after he greedily drinks from the chocolate stream and falls in.

"We thought one of the kids would get greedy and Mr. Wonka would kick them out. Were we right?" Emily's mom asks.

"Charlie was pretty good in the Chocolate Room," says Emily, "and we were right that one of the kids had to leave."

"But we didn't predict that Augustus would get sucked up into a pipe!"

"No, but he is greedy."

"Yes, and Charlie is the opposite of greedy."

In this conversation, Emily is using what she knows about the characters to discuss her predictions, and her mother extends the conversation to talk about the characters.

While inferencing involves making connections with sentences, paragraphs, and within books, children can also connect with fiction on a broader level, connecting with stories that allow them to either connect to our world or another world entirely.

What If My Child's Prediction Makes No Sense?

There are times when your child will make a prediction that seems to come from left field. This may not be a problem. As long as their prediction makes

Table 6.1. Inference and Prediction Questions

Inference Questions	Prediction Questions
Why do you think . . . ?	What do you think the story will be
What does this [picture, sentence] make you	about?
think?	What might happen if . . . ?
Why do they . . . ? How do you know?	What do you think will happen next?
Why do you think the author included that?	Why?
What probably caused . . . ?	
How might . . . feel . . . ?	

sense with the rest of the story, that's okay. For example, when Emily predicted that Charlie would "go crazy" in the Chocolate Room, that was aligned with Charlie's character, even if it wasn't exactly what happened. If Emily had predicted that Charlie would have wanted to leave the chocolate factory, that would have been incorrect, given that we know Charlie loves chocolate and really wanted to visit the factory.

Once your child makes a prediction, you can have a conversation about how their prediction could have been more accurate, once they find out what happened and think back on what clues the author gave that could have helped them. If their prediction is simply incorrect, go back in the book and reread any important part that can help them refine their prediction to make it more accurate. To do this, you can ask:

- What clues did the author give you that you could use?
- What clues did the author give us before? What did the character say or do that could have helped us see what was going to happen?

CONNECTING WITH STORIES TO LEARN ABOUT THE WORLD

Fiction is unique because it can immerse us in experiences that we cannot have in real life.[10] Think about the preschooler reading *The Snowy Day* by Ezra Jack Keats in the summer and connecting it to their experience of exploring their neighborhood after a snowstorm or other big weather event, about the third grader immersed in the imaginary world of Narnia in *The Lion, The Witch and the Wardrobe* by C. S. Lewis and "meeting" fawns and talking animals, or about an adult reader reading stories by Indian American author Jhumpa Lahiri and feeling the emotions that come with the experiences of the immigrant characters in her stories. Even children reading *Because of Winn-Dixie* by Kate DiCamillo and experiencing the adventures that Opal and Winn-Dixie have during their summer together are a way for children to experience something new through reading. All books, realistic and fantasy, immerse us in new worlds with interesting characters.

As we read fiction with children, we can help them connect and generalize what they learn from stories to their own experiences. This is the important learning that happens through connecting to fiction—children use information from stories to understand what happens in the real world.

Children as young as preschool can use the connections they make to picture books to better understand their experiences.[11] However, in elementary school, children read books that feature more complex situations and scenarios like bullying or dealing with difference or conflict. This is particularly true around the problems that characters face and the relationships that develop in stories. For example, a child who reads *Thank You, Mr. Falker* by Patricia Polacco, a story about a child who struggles to learn to read and is bullied because of it, can connect with the experience of struggling to do something that seems to come easily to everyone else. And they can talk about how to deal with bullies as a bystander and how to find and celebrate their friends' strengths.

As children become more aware of the different experiences that fiction provides, the way they connect to books develops. In short, connecting with stories helps kids experience empathy, which connects them to the stories and characters. This emotional investment helps them understand and remember what they read. For example, in *Thank You, Mr. Falker*, the child who struggles with reading will empathize with Trisha in a different way than a child who has not struggled with reading. But both children can talk about how to help someone who is struggling to learn or who is bullied.

Building empathy through reading is important. There has been a decrease in empathy among young people over the last two decades, most remarkably in the last ten years.[12] The need for empathy increases as we know more about the problems facing the world. The more empathy we have, and the better we can understand the perspective of others, the better we are at finding ways to deal with concerns and challenges in our own world.[13]

To help your child connect with a story and generalize information from the story to their own life, talk about the problem or scenario, what the character did, and what your child could do or has done in a similar situation. This encourages your child, first, to understand the scenario presented in the story, and then to take the perspective of the character to generalize the learning to their own life.

Caitlyn's dad reads Too Many Tamales *by Gary Soto, a story about a young girl who thinks that she has lost her mother's ring in the tamale dough and has to decide how to handle the situation. "What was Maria's problem in the story?" her dad asks.*

"She lost her mom's ring in the tamales."

Her dad turns to the page where Maria realizes that the ring is gone. *"She thought she lost the ring. What did she have to decide then?"*

"What to do."

"And what did she do?"

"First, she ate all the tamales, and then she told her mom the truth."

"Can you think of a time when you made a mistake?"

Caitlyn nods.

"How did you handle it?"

"I tried to hide it and then I told."

From this conversation, Caitlyn can talk through her experiences, especially thinking about those that she has struggled with. Her dad can help make the connections transparent by explaining what he sees in the book and connecting it with his own experiences. Through the conversation, her dad is able to talk about something that he wants Caitlyn to remember (how she has handled and could handle making mistakes) without lecturing or boring her.

USING FICTION TO HELP CHILDREN CONNECT TO TOUGH TOPICS

As children read, it's important for them to experience stories that reflect their own experience, as well as the experience of others (recall the windows and mirrors analogy in Chapter 3). When children make connections to stories and characters, they develop empathy, which deepens their understanding. Also, reading about an experience is one way of understanding that experience that children can take with them to better understand events and situations. For example, reading about Trisha's struggles in *Thank You, Mr. Falker* can help a child better relate to a friend who struggles with reading.

Stories can help children learn about tough topics, such as poverty, difference in race or ethnicity, facing adversity, and more. To help a child talk through a tough topic that you come across in a book, talk about what happened, provide reassurance where your child needs it, and talk about how your child feels and what they can learn from the story. Encourage your child to ask questions; even if you don't know the answer, the process of asking questions can lead to a deeper understanding of what we know and don't know about these topics. (There is a list of books that address tough topics in Appendix A.)

For example, the picture book *Last Stop on Market Street* by Matt de la Peña, a story about a boy who visits a soup kitchen with his grandmother, may raise questions about poverty, why neighborhoods look so different from

Table 6.2.   Stories about Common Experiences

Theme	Books	Questions to Ask
Friendship	*Enemy Pie* by Derek Munson *The Hundred Dresses* by Eleanor Estes *Charlotte's Web* by E. B. White *Each Kindness* by Jacqueline Woodson	How would you describe the character? What did the character want? How did they go about getting what they wanted? What happened to the character? What did they do? What would you do if that happened to you?
Conflict in Relationships	*Best Friends for Frances* by Russell Hoban *The Recess Queen* by Alexis O'Neill *Stand Tall, Molly Lou Melon* by Patty Lovell *The Invisible Boy* by Trudy Ludwig *The Sandwich Swap* by Queen Rania of Jordan	What happened to the character? How did it make them feel? How did they respond? Has anything like that ever happened to you? What did you do?
Being Yourself	*Chrysanthemum* by Kevin Henkes *Leo the Late Bloomer* by Robert Kraus *Tacky the Penguin* by Helen Lester *A Bad Case of Stripes* by David Shannon *Julián Is a Mermaid* by Jessica Love *I Am Enough* by Grace Byers *The Name Jar* by Yangsook Choi	How was the character unique? Have you ever felt unique? What do you think is unique about you? How did the character handle being different? How did the character feel? Have you ever felt that way?
Strong Emotions	*Wemberly Worried* by Kevin Henkes *Alexander and the Terrible, Horrible, No Good, Very Bad Day* by Judith Viorst *Those Shoes* by Maribeth Boelts *Life without Nico* by Andrea Maturana *The Snurtch* by Sean Ferrell	What happened to the character? How did he feel? Have you ever felt that way? What happened? How did you deal with it? What would you tell the character? What could he do?

one another, and why people eat at soup kitchens. From this, first, you can ask what happened to CJ and his grandma in the story. Then connect the story to your child's experiences and feelings: Has your child ever experienced anything like volunteering at a soup kitchen? Have they ever helped someone who seemed to have less? What did it feel like? How does the story make your child feel?

Take the conversation further by asking more specific questions about the story: What does CJ do in the story? How does he help? And connect to what your child could do to address the topic, in this case people who are hungry in your community, by talking about what you could do or making a plan to help.

The point of reading stories that tackle tough topics is not just to develop empathy, although that is an important outcome, but also to empower your child to understand what happens in the world, how it can be addressed, and what they can do when they encounter a tough problem.

CONNECT TO YOUR CHILD'S WORLD

The *C* in the ABCs of Active Reading is particularly important for early elementary schoolers. At the most basic level, making connections helps children make inferences, a basic comprehension skill. It also helps them broaden their understanding of how the world works and their role in it, and how they understand and engage with important problems.

Children connect with fiction stories to learn about how their world works. They connect with nonfiction to learn facts and knowledge. Chapter 7 covers how to help children build background knowledge and use that knowledge to better understand nonfiction.

* * *

WHAT TO REMEMBER

- When we make inferences, we take what we know and add new information to create new meaning or a deeper understanding. The ability to make inferences while reading is important for comprehension. As children learn to read, they need lots of practice making inferences to become adept at it.
- There are two types of basic inferences:
  - Cause-and-effect inferences, when readers make a connection between an initial event and its consequence
  - Relationship inferences, when readers integrate information across a text to make inferences that support their understanding of the story
- You can help make inferencing a habit for your child by talking about new information that comes into what you are reading and, over time, asking them questions that help them make the inferences on their own.
- A prediction is an inference specifically about what will happen next in the story. When children make predictions, they are demonstrating what

they understand by using what they have already read to anticipate new information in the story. To help your child make a prediction, you can ask a series of questions:

- ○ What do you think will happen next?
- ○ What in the story makes you think that?
- As long as a prediction makes sense, it isn't wrong. The important thing is to circle back on the predictions you make and talk about whether they were right and wrong and, if they were wrong, what information they could have used from the story to anticipate what actually happened.
- Fiction provides us with the experience of reading about imaginary experiences that relate to those we have in real life. Reading fiction also builds empathy, an important component in helping children connect and relate to others and the world.
- To help your child connect with a book and generalize information from the story to their own life, talk about the problem or scenario, what the character did, and what your child could do or has done in a similar situation.

Making Connections to Nonfiction Text

When Stephanie Six was in elementary school, horses were her passion. She read every horse story she could get her hands on (*Misty of Chincoteague, King of the Wind, The Black Stallion*). She grew up in the suburbs, so fiction was a way for Stephanie to experience what it was like to own a horse or be a horse.

Nonfiction was how Stephanie learned about the ins and outs of horses. The technical terms (*fetlock, mane, withers*). She also studied encyclopedias about horses to learn about the breeds and how they are colored. She pored over diagrams to learn about Arabian horses and make sure she could recognize Clydesdales. She particularly remembers studying Arabian horses, learning why their heads are shaped how they are, their size, how fast they can run. She also learned about other topics as she read about horses. Reading about the Spanish Riding School taught her about daily life in Vienna and classic horsemanship elements, like dressage (a type of horse dancing).

Stephanie's interest in horses was the entry point to reading lots of nonfiction. Think back to a topic you were interested in as a child—dinosaurs, animals, outer space, horses.

- How did you learn about it?
- How did you learn the specific vocabulary and concepts?

Erin Pavon, mom to six-year-old twins and a five-year-old, reads the *Ordinary People Change the World* books to her boys to teach them about Amelia Earhart, Martin Luther King Jr., and other historical figures. The series deals with real-world, adult themes, says Pavon. Each book explains the context for each famous person with just enough information that her boys understand, but doesn't scare or worry them. "We try to use books as tools for explaining important lessons and other things that are going on in the world," says Pavon.

Beyond connecting the kids with themes and lessons, nonfiction books can also introduce and teach kids about their interests, like one son's excitement for robots and another's interest in sea creatures. Sharing nonfiction books as read-alouds helps Pavon give her kids information about what they're interested in using books they're not able to read on their own yet (recall the importance of reading deeply from Chapter 3).

Books that explain and explore real-life topics, from the ocean floor to the human body, are a natural draw for young children who are interested in understanding the world around them. Nonfiction has become a focus of reading curriculum and classroom libraries in recent years because children were not engaging with nonfiction texts enough.[1] One study found that less than 9 percent of the books read to early elementary–age children were nonfiction.[2] Another analysis of first-grade classrooms found that informational texts made up less than 10 percent of the books in classroom libraries (9.8 percent) and that children spent an average of 3.6 minutes with informational text each day.[3] This is important because the early elementary years are a crucial time for developing foundational knowledge of the world and how things work.

In general, children like reading nonfiction,[4] which is good because nonfiction teaches background knowledge and academic vocabulary (words about a specific topic, like the words *meteor*, *asteroid*, and *planet* in a book about the solar system). Later, background knowledge and vocabulary help children learn about a topic through reading. In fact, children's background knowledge accounts for as much as 33 percent of the variance in student achievement,[5] meaning that student success in reading in general can be traced back to their background knowledge.

Early elementary school is also a time when children are learning how texts work, and nonfiction texts have a different structure than fiction, so lots of exposure to informational text builds children's understanding of the many ways that authors can present information. Through reading and discussion, children can learn reading comprehension skills that are specific to nonfiction.[6] For example, reading about how a scientist identified and solved a problem teaches children how to understand a problem and solution structure.

Reading nonfiction books with your child is a great way to encourage your child to explore topics they're interested in and build background knowledge, all while teaching them how to use books to learn about anything and everything. As children progress through school, they'll gain more and more knowledge from books. This chapter focuses on how to engage your child in Active Reading using nonfiction picture books.

NONFICTION AND THIRD-GRADE READING

When it comes to reading, third grade is a pivotal year for kids. When children have a solid foundation in reading skills and are reading well by third grade, they are well on their way to successful school experiences, graduation, and beyond.[7] Third grade is the point when, it's often said, children shift from "learning to read" to "reading to learn."

That is an important distinction. In grades K–2 children are learning the foundational skills of reading (see Chapter 2). By the time children leave third grade, they are learning to use books to understand and learn new information. Think about the shift from picture books and easy readers about a topic to content-specific textbooks that have much more information.

In the upper grades, children will learn how to read longer and more complex words (also called *multisyllabic words*), build their vocabulary, and practice comprehension strategies for longer, more difficult texts. However, as children transition into upper elementary school, they will have to do more reading to learn, or they will be given a text and asked to do something with it—prepare for a discussion, learn about a topic, and explain it to peers—without as much teacher support to sound out words and read fluently.

Of course, there is an important caveat: children are "reading to learn" before third grade and they will be learning reading comprehension strategies long before third grade as well.[8] The big difference between early elementary (grades K–3) and upper elementary (grades 4–8) is the expectation around what children are asked to do with their reading skills. In general, in upper elementary, teachers expect students to have word reading and fluency skills, so they can apply their reading ability to new stories and nonfiction texts.

Beyond background knowledge and vocabulary, there are some other benefits to reading lots of nonfiction. In particular, it can motivate young readers by igniting their interests and letting them explore books directly related to what they are interested in.[9] As children move through elementary school, nonfiction texts become increasingly relevant.

THE CHALLENGE OF READING NONFICTION

Nonfiction may not be the mainstay of early elementary reading, but it is important and engaging. There are unique features of nonfiction that make it more difficult to read than fiction, namely, background knowledge, text structure, and academic vocabulary.

Background Knowledge

The more you know about a topic, the easier it is to read about it. You may have seen this in your own life as you delved into a new topic for work or fun. For example, reading about the Apollo 11 moon landing is easier if you have a general knowledge of the who (Buzz Aldrin, Neil Armstrong, NASA), when (1969), and what (the Americans landed a lunar module on the moon for the first time). Even that basic knowledge makes it easier to connect new information about the event to build meaning from a newspaper article or book. This is the same for children, who have much less background knowledge about the world than adults do. Sometimes, books do a great job of helping set the stage for comprehension with lots of basic information about a topic (think: the who, what, when, where, why). Other times, a book may start assuming that the reader knows at least the basics and not give as much information.

That's not to say that you should not read about topics that you don't know well. Rather, when you don't know much about a topic, you'll start reading about it differently than if you would read about something you already know about. For example, if you do not know anything about horses, you may read general books about horses and how to take care of them. Then, once you know more, you can delve into books about the specific breeds, horse events, and more in-depth information about horses.

Text Structure

There are lots of different ways to explore a topic. You could use a simple explanation like *This Is How We Do It* by Matt Lamothe, a picture book that explains and shows how seven children live around the world. You could use a compare-and-contrast structure, like *Frog or Toad? How Do You Know?* by Melissa Stewart, which compares the characteristics of the two animals. Or you could use a story format like *The Noisy Paint Box* by Barb Rosenstock, a biography of the artist Kandinsky. Each of these books have a different way of presenting information, based on what the author wants the reader to learn and be thinking about as they read.

When children are not aware of text structure, they aren't able to anticipate how the text will present information. When they do know about text structure and how to use it, they can anticipate and better comprehend nonfiction.[10] Children often arrive at school with an understanding of how fiction works simply from being read to at home. In school, they must advance their understanding of text structure as they learn how to read nonfiction and as they learn to read to learn new things[11] (more on text structure later in this chapter).

Academic Vocabulary

Finally, academic vocabulary, or words that are specific to a topic, are a challenge as a child learns about the topic. In the book *Wonder Horse: The True Story of the World's Smartest Horse* by Emily McCully, the words *plantation* and *liniment* relate to the historical period. The words *stallion*, *foal*, and *Arabian* relate to the topic of horses. In *The Big Book of Beasts* by Yuval Zommer, words like *mammal*, *primates*, *carnivores*, and *marsupials* extend children's knowledge of the animal world. Children must be able to define words while they read and use text features (captions, definitions in the text, glossaries) to understand words. (Academic vocabulary is also discussed in Chapter 5.)

BACKGROUND KNOWLEDGE: THE BACKBONE FOR UNDERSTANDING NONFICTION

Nina and her mom are reading Lost and Found Cat: The True Story of Kunkush's Incredible Journey *by Doug Kuntz and Amy Shrodes, a story about a cat that got separated from his family during their escape from Iraq through Greece to Norway.*

"Did you know that people are leaving Iraq because of war?" her mom asks her.

"No, where is Iraq?"

Her mom turns to the map at the back of the book. "This is Iraq." She traces the line that shows the route the family took. "And they had to cross a sea to get to Greece and then they went all the way to Norway. When someone leaves their homeland because of war or because they are in danger, they are refugees."

Nina's mom is building background knowledge about geography and refugees that will help Nina understand the story. Background knowledge, or the amount of knowledge that a child has about a topic, affects how well they understand what they read about it.[12] Put another way, the more you know about something, the easier it is to understand and remember new information about it. The importance of background knowledge emerges as early as preschool, meaning that young children are using background knowledge to understand and make sense of new things that they learn, in this case through reading aloud.[13]

It's important for us to have background knowledge both to understand new information when we read, and to integrate new information with what we know to make inferences as we read.[14] Specifically, background knowledge helps readers better understand words and phrases, make inferences, and think about what they read.

- ***Understanding words:*** Background knowledge helps us make decisions about which meaning a word can have and choose the right word in context.[15] For example, reading a cookbook, you'd understand the word *sharp* to refer to a knife. Reading a medical textbook, you'd know that a *sharp* was a needle. Words have various meanings that change depending on the context, and how a word is used is cued or prompted by the context and by the child's knowledge.
- ***Making inferences:*** Reading requires making inferences (Chapter 6), and reading comprehension relies on making lots of accurate inferences as we read. Background knowledge helps us make accurate inferences. If we do not have an understanding of the topic, we can get caught in the "seductive details," or the interesting and entertaining information that is not directly related to a topic, rather than engaging in the topic itself.[16] In other words, we lose sight of the important information for the unimportant details or fun facts when we don't have enough background knowledge to recognize and weed out less important information.

Build Background Knowledge: Read Wide and Deep

There are two ways to build lots of background knowledge through reading: reading wide and deep (also covered in Chapter 3). Recall that when we read wide, we read about lots of different topics, and when we read deep, we read a lot about one topic. For example, your child may read a selection of *Magic School Bus* books about topics from dinosaurs to outer space to the human body. As they do this, they're building knowledge about each topic, and more generally how the world works. If they find one of those books particularly interesting, the book about outer space, for example, they may read lots of books about outer space: *Space: For Kids Who Really Love Space!* by Roger Priddy, *National Geographic Kids Little Kids First Big Book of Space* by

Catherine Hughes, and *Star Stuff: Carl Sagan and the Mysteries of the Cosmos* by Stephanie Roth Sisson. Now they're reading deeply about one topic.

How to Encourage Wide and Deep Reading

There are things you can do to encourage your child to read both wide and deep:

- When your child finds a topic that they are interested in, get a combination of books that they can read on their own and books that you read together so that you can use Active Reading to help them build knowledge and encourage conversation, but they can still read about the topic on their own.
- As your child reads, compare and contrast new information with information you know they have about the topic. Ask:
  ○ What did you learn?
  ○ What was new for you?
  ○ What did you already know about?
- Write your own questions. Write down questions you have about the topic, things you wonder, and facts that surprise you.
- Go beyond the book. Visit museums, explore online resources, watch documentaries or movies about the topic. Extending your child's interest in a topic helps them apply what they learned to new contexts.

TALK ABOUT NONFICTION BOOK STRUCTURE

Olivia and her dad are reading Wonder Horse *by Emily McCully.*

"This story takes place a long time ago," her dad says. "Bill Key was born in 1833; that's a long time ago. And I can see the clothes they're wearing are a lot different than what we wear."

They continue reading and learn more about the story of Bill Key and his horse, Jim, which Key taught to identify colors and letters. "This book is reading like a story," Olivia's dad notices. "There is a beginning and middle and end."

"And a problem," Olivia adds.

"What's the problem?"

"That Bill wants Jim to show what he can do."

"Yes, the author is telling the story of someone's life, that's called a biography. *Biographies are often read like stories."*

One of the interesting things about nonfiction is how it's organized. Text structure is how the ideas in a text are organized and how the ideas connect to one another.[17] Talking about how texts are organized helps children understand that texts can have different structures and that those structures help us understand more from each text. When children understand how a nonfiction text is organized, and can anticipate that while they're reading, they can use that knowledge to understand what they're reading about as well.[18] On the other hand, there are multiple ways to organize a text, so readers must put more effort into comprehending the text. And children must develop a knowledge of text structures in order to use it.

There are a variety of ways to organize text, including:

- **Description:** An author describes a process or what is happening. For example, *So You Want to Be President?* by Judith St. George and David Small is a book that describes the aspects of the presidency, how people become president, and what presidents have done throughout history. The *You Wouldn't Want to . . .* book series describes life without or with a certain thing, such as *You Wouldn't Want to Live without Math* by Anne Rooney. Some books describe one type of animal, system, or phenomenon, like *What the Moon Is Like* by Franklyn Branley (one of many books in the *Let's Read and Find Out* series).
- **Sequence:** When an author uses an order (numerical, chronological) to explain an event, this includes biographies and historical stories, such as *Worst of Friends: Thomas Jefferson, John Adams, and the True Story of an American Feud* by Suzanne Jurmain and *Counting on Katherine: How Katherine Johnson Saved Apollo 13* by Helaine Becker.
- **Compare and contrast:** This structure is used when an author compares and contrasts two or more events, topics, people, and so forth. Authors can compare and contrast people in history, such as *Aaron and Alexander: The Most Famous Duel in American History* by Don Brown or two types of animals like *Butterfly or Moth?* by Melissa Stewart.
- **Cause and effect:** This structure is used to describe events or processes that result from one another, such as *Aliens from Earth: When Animals and Plants Invade Other Ecosystems* by Mary Batten or *The Reasons for Seasons* by Gail Gibbons about how the earth's rotation causes the seasons.
- **Problem and solution:** This structure is used when a problem or question is posed and a solution is given. An example is *The Right Word: Roget and His Thesaurus* by Jen Bryant and Melissa Sweet. Many historical stories also have a problem-and-solution structure, such as *Brave Girl: Clara and the Shirtwaist Makers' Strike of 1909* by Michelle Markel and *Separate Is Never Equal: Sylvia Mendez and Her Family's Fight for Desegregation* by Duncan Tonatiuh.

Table 7.1. Books by Text Structure

Text Structure	Description	Book Examples
Description	The author provides a description of a topic or idea.	*Your Fantastic Elastic Brain* by JoAnn Deak *So You Want to Be President?* by Judith St. George *The Pumpkin Book* by Gail Gibbons
Sequence	The author provides an account of an event in chronological, or time, order. Keywords: *first, then, next*	*Pop! The Invention of Bubble Gum* by Meghan McCarthy *A Raindrop's Journey* by Suzanne Slade *Whoosh! Lonnie Johnson's Super-Soaking Stream of Inventions* by Chris Barton
Compare and contrast	The author compares two things, saying what is similar and different about them. Keywords: *but, in comparison*	*Aaron and Alexander: The Most Famous Duel in American History* by Don Brown *Poles Apart* by Jeanne Willis *Now and Ben: The Modern Inventions of Benjamin Franklin* by Gene Barretta
Cause and effect	The author shows how one thing caused another to happen. Keywords: *first, then, as a result*	*The Reason for a Flower* by Ruth Heller *Flash, Crash, Rumble, and Roll* by Franklyn Branley *Animals That Changed the World* by Keltie Thomas
Problem and solution	The author describes a problem and how it was solved.	*A Place for Butterflies* by Melissa Stewart *The Boy Who Harnessed the Wind* by William Kamkwamba *The Right Word: Roget and His Thesaurus* by Jen Bryant

Text Features

Nicholas and his mother are reading See inside Your Body *by Katie Daynes, a book about the human body.*

"Wow, there are a lot of diagrams in this book," his mom notes.

"What are diagrams?" Nicholas asks.

"Diagrams are pictures that have words to tell you what they show."

They examine a diagram of the circulatory system. Nicholas follows the diagram from the heart through arteries and veins. As he does, his mom reads the various parts of the system, and they talk about what each does.

Another aspect of nonfiction that is important are text features, things like headings, captions, glossaries, even maps, and images. Having an understanding of text features is important when students read text on their own.[19] For example, understanding that headings tell us about what the section is going to be about can help readers locate information in a text, which can help children start making connections between what they know and what they are going to learn. Reading the captions in photos gives readers more information about the images, and how they add to the other information. Before you read a nonfiction book, scan through and identify various text features, like pictures, charts, and graphs. Use these to think about what you already know about the topic and wonder about what you'll learn.

Table 7.2.　Text Features in Nonfiction

Text Feature	What It Is	How It Helps You Understand What You Read
Table of Contents	The list of chapters or topics in the start of the book	Helps you find key topics in the book and shows how the book is organized.
Caption	Text under a picture or photograph	Helps you understand what the image is about and may add details to what the book is about.
Glossary	A list of words with definitions in the back of the book	Helps you define words that are important for that book.
Graphics	Charts, graphics, maps, diagrams	Show what the author is trying to explain.
Images	Illustrations or photographs	Show what something looks like.
Index	An alphabetical list of ideas in the book	Help you find where certain information is located in the book.
Labels	Text that explain graphics or images	Help you understand the diagram or image.

APPLYING THE ABCS OF ACTIVE READING TO NONFICTION

When Elizabeth Meyer, age nine, and her dad read a nonfiction book about scientific discoveries throughout history, they talked about penicillin and how Alexander Fleming was able to change modern medicine and save lives from the mold he found on bacteria samples. After reading the book and talking about it, they inspected all the cheese in the refrigerator to look for mold. Elizabeth's dad engaged her in conversation and immediately connected the information to her world, building background knowledge of penicillin and how we generate discoveries.

Active Reading with nonfiction is similar to Active Reading with any other book—you're still asking questions, building vocabulary, and making connections. There are a few specifics to consider and some unique ways to approach nonfiction, which can include more text features, like pictures, graphics, charts, and photos. As your child gets to know nonfiction, they may not realize that what they're reading is true and may need help orienting themselves to the topic.

Getting Started: Book Walks

When we read fiction, we may start with a picture walk to preview the story. For nonfiction, the same basic idea is a book walk. Flip through the book before you read it and get a sense for what you'll read about. Talk about how this book tells us about a real-life topic and talk about what you already know about the topic, or where you've learned about it before. Before you read a book about dinosaurs, have you been to a museum exhibit about dinosaurs? Or before reading a book about the ocean, have you been to the beach? Talk about any experiences that your child has had, including TV shows and other books that are about this topic. This will help activate their background knowledge by reminding them that they can connect new information to their existing knowledge.

Read through the table of contents, glossary, index, charts, and other text features. Talk about what each item does in this book:

- What does the photo show?
- What does the caption of the photo tell you?
- What does the chart tell us?
- Do they see anything in the table of contents or index that they want to learn more about? Feel free to start there instead of the first page.

Ask Questions about Nonfiction

Claire and her dad are reading The Big Book of Beasts *by Yuval Zommer.*

"This book gives us a lot of information," her dad says. They turn to a page about tigers. "What's interesting to you about tigers?" her dad asks before reading the page about tigers.

"They are carnivores," says Claire.

"I wonder how they take care of their babies," her dad muses.

They read the page, with facts about tiger spit, its weight, how they take care of their cubs, and more.

"What did you learn?" her dad asks before they turn the page.

"I didn't know that the tiger can heal itself with its spit," says Claire.

A few big things to talk about with nonfiction are structure and topic. As mentioned earlier, text structure is not obvious to young readers; we have to talk about what the text is telling us and how it's organized. This helps children start understanding that authors organize text with a plan and that we can understand how nonfiction can be organized. Also, your child is reading a nonfiction book to learn more about the topic, whether that's George Washington or how seeds grow, so you'll want to talk about what the book is about and what they're learning.

Think about asking questions before, during, and after reading to help your child understand the text structure, and use that knowledge to better understand the content.

Before Reading

- What type of book is this?
  - Is it going to describe something?
  - Do you think you'll learn about how to classify or describe something?
  - Do you think you'll read about a problem and solution?
- Use the title, cover, and table of contents, and flip through the book to look at the pictures for information about the text structure. Look for text features that can help you build background knowledge and create questions about what the book is about.
- Ask your child what questions they have. Their questions may align with the type of structure they're going to be reading. For example, they may ask, "What happened?" before reading a biography or "What do we know about?" before reading a descriptive text.

During Reading

- Talk about changes in the text. These could be parts when something new is introduced, like a new idea, a change in the opinion of the author, or the next bit of information in a chronological book. You can ask:
  - What happened next?
  - How did that change things?
- For books that have a sequential text structure, talk about what happened in order: first, second, and so on.
- For books that have a descriptive structure, talk about what you learned about that topic:
  - What information was new?
  - What did you learn?

After Reading

- Talk about what your child took away from the text by asking:
  - What did you learn?
  - What do you think about this topic?
  - What could you share with a friend?
- Look back and talk about the structure now that you've read it:

- ○ What did the author do?
- ○ In a sequential book, what events did the author pull out?
- ○ In a description, what did the author think was important to include?
- ○ In cause and effect, was the effect positive or negative?
- ○ In problem and solution, how did they solve the problem and can we learn anything from this story?

The point of talking about text structure is not to memorize types of text structure (your child's teacher will cover text structure more in depth in school). Rather, use the structure as a way to organize your own thinking and conversation about the information in the book. The best way to encourage your child to be an Active Reader with nonfiction is to show them how you think about nonfiction as you read. Talk out loud as you look at the pages in the book and read:

- What are you wondering?
- What questions does the book make you think about?
- What surprises do you find in the text?
- What new information is there for you?
- What connections are you making?

Thinking aloud like this shows your child how readers think as they read.

Building Vocabulary with Nonfiction

Reading the page in The Big Book of Beasts *about lions, Claire's dad stops at the word* lioness. *"Do you know what a lioness is?" he asks.*

Claire shakes her head.

"It's a female lion. Like a female deer is called a doe, *there is a word for female lions."*

"I wonder why there are different words for male and female lions," Claire wonders.

"I don't know," her dad says. "What do you think?"

Nonfiction books often contain more academic vocabulary compared to fiction.[20] We know that Active Reading can develop vocabulary, and this applies to academic vocabulary as well.[21] We teach new words the same way we build vocabulary with fiction, with a focus on how the word connects to the topic we're reading about. (Chapter 6 has more information about how to teach words through Active Reading.)

Make Connections to Nonfiction

Connecting what your child already knows to what they are learning from books is an important way to help them learn. To do this, ask questions that help connect to other experiences or texts that your child has read about the topic, like, "Does this remind you of anything else we've read about?"

In The Big Book of Beasts, *Claire and her father connect new information about hyenas, tigers, and lions to what they learned at the zoo and on television shows about animals. Claire points out that she knew that hyenas eat every part of the animals they kill, but she did not know that the noise hyenas make are how they communicate with their pack.*

As we make connections with nonfiction, ask:

- What do you already know about this?
- What is new information?
- What did you learn?
- What else do you want to know?

Connecting here is all about helping your child interact with the book to build knowledge and set the stage to learn even more.

CONNECT WITH NONFICTION TEXT

Your child may have a preference for fiction or nonfiction. However, spending time reading nonfiction text together gives you an opportunity to show your child how interesting nonfiction can be and how many different types of nonfiction there are, and preparing them to enjoy reading to learn about what interests them. You're selling your child on nonfiction, if you will. As you do this, you're preparing them for the increased demands of reading as they advance through school. Chapter 8 explores how to engage your child in another new reading experience for elementary schoolers, chapter books and novels.

* * *

WHAT TO REMEMBER

- Reading nonfiction in elementary grades builds background knowledge and vocabulary, two important aspects for general reading comprehension, and is motivating for kids.

- It can be more challenging to read nonfiction than fiction because of the background knowledge that is needed, the academic vocabulary, and the text structure.
- Background knowledge about a topic helps readers better understand words and phrases in a book, make inferences, and think about what they read. We build background knowledge by reading widely and deeply.
- Nonfiction books have lots of academic vocabulary. Children must use the text to understand those words as they relate to the topic.
- Text structure is how the information in a book is organized and how the ideas connect to one another. When children know how a book is organized, they can use that information to understand what they read.
- There are various ways to organize nonfiction, but some common ones are description, sequence, compare and contrast, cause and effect, and problem and solution.
- Text features, like images, glossaries, and more, are important for children to use when they are reading to understand the information in books.
- Active Reading with nonfiction is similar to Active Reading with fiction in that you are still doing the ABCs and having a conversation about the book.
- When you ask questions while reading nonfiction, talk about the type of book, how the information is organized, what your child is learning, and what is new to them.
- Building vocabulary with nonfiction means learning new academic vocabulary words that are specific to the topic.
- Making connections with nonfiction involves connecting to your child's knowledge about the topic and extending their thinking to learn even more.

8

Active Reading with Chapter Books and Novels

Kate Meyer started reading chapter books to her oldest daughter, Elizabeth, when she was in preschool. During a visit to the library, Elizabeth found one of the *Rainbow Magic* books by Daisy Meadows, a series of short, illustrated chapter books about two girls who save fairies from an evil goblin. Elizabeth insisted on bringing it home. That was Elizabeth's first experience with chapter books and she was hooked. Through preschool and kindergarten, Meyer read lots of different picture books and early readers with the occasional *Rainbow Magic* chapter book. Then, in first grade, Elizabeth started asking for more chapter books and fewer picture books.

Now Meyer has a stack of chapter books that her daughters (ages nine and six) have enjoyed reading with both her and her husband. Over the past year, recalls Meyer, her husband has read their kids the *Diary of a Wimpy Kid* books by Jeff Kinney. Reading *Diary of a Wimpy Kid* is fun for her husband and the girls. "I am convinced that the allure for them is how hard their dad laughs while reading them," says Meyer.

They also find themselves returning to familiar series, like *The Boxcar Children* by Gertrude Chandler Warner, a series of mysteries undertaken by the four Alden siblings. "We take breaks for other books, but always find ourselves back to the stories of the Alden siblings," says Meyer. Thinking about *The Boxcar Children*, specifically, one of the reasons that Kate loves reading them to her oldest is that, even now that the series is below her reading level (Elizabeth can read the books easily on her own), the mysteries in the books always lead to conversations. They talk about the setting, hypothesize about the characters, who is responsible, and predict how the regular characters will respond to each new problem.

Think about the reading you've done with your child so far:

- What is your child's "diet" of picture books, chapter books, and other books?
- If you do read chapter books aloud, what has gone well?
- If you haven't read a chapter book or novel aloud, would you like to?
  - What would you like to gain from reading chapter books aloud?
  - Is there anything that has stopped you from choosing a chapter book for reading aloud?

In the *Sofia Martinez* series by Jacqueline Jules, Sofia has everyday, kid-sized problems—wanting to find an audience for her new karaoke machine, having to clean up her mother's flower garden after flooding it with a hose—that she has to figure her way out of. This is a great introduction to chapter books because the chapters are short (there are about three chapters per story and multiple stories per book). The stories are clear with basic story grammar and just enough new words (Jules has incorporated Spanish words throughout the books) to engage young readers. It also has some of the characteristics of chapter books that young readers like: multiple chapters and a length that you have to put down and come back to.

Chapter books are the bridge between easy readers, books they have less text and more pictures, and novels, when the entire story is text with longer chapters and more complex stories. Chapter books have longer stories, broken into chapters, but often have illustrations, and simpler stories than novels. As milestones go, there is the first time you read a chapter book aloud to your child, the first time they read a chapter book on their own, and the first time they discover a chapter book series they really like. Then there is the first real novel your child reads, and the first time you tackle a longer novel together.

For kids, chapter books and novels are a rite of passage. When they can read a chapter book on their own, they've progressed far enough in their reading that they can tackle a longer book with fewer pictures. In fact, reading chapter books, like *Lulu's Animal Adventures* by Hilary McKay, *Stink!* by Megan McDonald, or *Junie B. Jones* by Barbara Park, on their own, is something that children should be doing by the end of first grade or the beginning of second grade. When they're reading chapter books on their own, they are getting close to "grown-up" reading.

Active Reading can help your child make the leap from easy readers to chapter books and then novels by building the stamina, language, and understanding of story grammar needed to understand longer reads. We've already covered reading aloud in general, with examples from chapter books and novels, but this specific type of text demands some extra attention. In this chapter we discuss choosing chapter books to read together and for your child to read on their own, and how to apply the ABCs of Active Reading to chapter books and novels.

WHAT MAKES CHAPTER BOOKS AND NOVELS SPECIAL?

When we read longer books, we have to carry our knowledge across the entire text, whether it's ten pages or one thousand pages. That's the biggest difference between a picture book and a chapter book: the story is usually read in multiple sessions, so your child has to remember information from one reading to the next.

As your child becomes confident with early readers, they can transition into chapter books, which usually happens around age seven or eight. Chapter books, even illustrated ones, also have fewer illustrations than picture books. Recall that pictures help your child understand what is happening in the story. This means that children must create more of the image of what the author is writing when they read chapter books. Creating their own mental imagery is an important step as children shift from using illustrations to build meaning to visualizing a story on their own.

Your child will encounter two types of chapter books: the first you'll read together and the second they'll read on their own. You'll know your child is ready to listen to chapter books when they can follow longer picture books with longer, more complex stories, like books by Patricia Polacco or Kevin Henkes (see Appendix A). Or they may be ready when they pull a chapter book off the shelf and ask to bring it home, as Meyer's daughter did with the *Rainbow Magic* books. There's no specific age when kids will read chapter books; some children will be ready to listen to chapter books sooner than others (and there's no benefit to pushing longer books earlier than when the child is ready).

Choosing Chapter Books and Novels to Read Together

That first chapter book that your child listens to can seem like an important one. Will it be captivating enough to catapult them into the world of chapter books? Will it be engaging enough to keep their attention across multiple sessions? Will the character be lovable enough to encourage your child to read more?

The good news: children who love reading are rarely turned off by one negative book or reading experience. So if you choose a book and your child doesn't like it, move on to the next. You can also tell them that it's okay if they don't like a book. If they're reading for fun, they should be having fun and if they're not, put the book down and move on to the next one (Table 8.1). When you are choosing chapter books to read together, think about:

- Your child's interests.
- Your child's attention span; are they able to listen to longer chapters or do they need to work with shorter chapters?
- What your child has already experienced and whether they have background knowledge they can use to understand the story. For example, children who have attended formal school will have more background knowledge to understand *Matilda* by Roald Dahl than those who haven't.
- The language in the book. Some classic chapter books (*Charlotte's Web* and *Stuart Little* by E. B. White, *Paddington* by Michael Bond, *Pippi Longstocking* by Astrid Lindgren) and even modern classics (*Beezus and Ramona* or *Socks* by Beverly Cleary) use language that is too formal for today's young children to understand without clarification.
- The genre of the book. Realistic fiction is great for young children because they can relate it to their everyday life, while historical fiction may escape them (e.g., the *Dear America* series may be better for older children with more knowledge about the world or with an interest in history). Your child may like books that show real kids more than fantasy stories, or vice versa.

Table 8.1.   First Chapter Books

Great Chapter Books to Start With	Great Chapter Books to Read Next
Mercy Watson (series) by Kate DiCamillo	Toys Go Out by Emily Jenkins
Dory Fantasmagory books by Abby Hanlon	Fantastic Mr. Fox by Roald Dahl
Lotta on Troublemaker Street by Astrid Lindgren	James and the Giant Peach by Roald Dahl
Princess in Black books by Shannon Hale	Charlie and the Chocolate Factory by Roald Dahl
Lulu's Animal Adventure series by Hilary McKay	The Cricket in Times Square by George Selden
Sofia Martinez books by Jaqueline Jules	Charlotte's Web by E. B. White
Anna Hibiscus books by Atinuke	Stuart Little by E. B. White
Sherlock Sam books by A. J. Low	The Whipping Boy by Sid Fleischman
Bobby the Brave books by Lisa Yee	The Tale of Despereaux by Kate DiCamillo
Yasmin books by Saadia Faruqi	Because of Winn-Dixie by Kate DiCamillo
	The One and Only Ivan by Katherine Applegate
	Dyamonde Daniel series by Nikki Grimes
	Jake the Fake Keeps It Real by Craig Robinson and Adam Mansbach
	Stone Fox by John Reynolds Gardiner

If your child is not interested in a chapter book you choose, put it away until they do have the interest or background knowledge to engage with it. (It's okay if they never return to that book; they don't have to read all the books out there!) If it is a book that is meaningful for you and you really want to read it with them, build their background knowledge by doing activities or taking them places, or reading picture books that will help get them there.

For example, you may have read *The Chronicles of Narnia* by C. S. Lewis when you were younger, but find that your children aren't able to follow the plot (or aren't interested in the story). It's okay to put the chapter books away, and read the picture book (written by C. S. Lewis and Tudor Humphries) to introduce your children to the basic story, characters (Lucy and her siblings, Aslan, and the White Witch), and genre. After engaging with the story in another way, your child may be eager to return to the chapter books. And even if they're not, they can still share the story with you.

Choosing Chapter Books for Your Child to Read on Their Own

Your child's first chapter book will likely be an extension of the easy reader books they are already reading, but with short chapters that combine to tell a story. It may be a book with multiple stories, like *Little Bear* by Else Minarik that helps young readers build stamina, or the ability to read pages with more words on a page and in a sentence and paragraph. From there, your child may discover a character, like *Junie B. Jones* by Barbara Park or *Nate the Great* by Marjorie Sharmat, or a genre, like the *A to Z Mysteries* by Ron Roy or *Geronimo Stilton* by Geronimo Stilton. However your child discovers their first chapter book, you can make sure it's a good fit by teaching them a few techniques to choose books that are good for them as they ease into chapter books they can read on their own:

1. Look at the cover, title, and back cover to see what's interesting about the book and what they may already know that would help them read it. For example, have they read a book about this character before? Also, how interested are they in reading it? They may be very motivated to read about a character their teacher has talked about, or to find out what their friends are reading.
2. Read the summary on the back of the book. Does the summary make them want to read the story?
3. Scan the text. Does it look like text they can read, with just enough words on each page?

4. Read the first page or so to get a feel for whether they can read most of the words (reading nine out of ten words correctly is a rough estimate).

From there, decide if it's a book they want to read. You may find that a book you thought was too complicated, with longer words and more complex sentences, is a perfect challenge for a motivated child, or that a book that seemed too easy at first glance (maybe you thought there were too many pictures) is so engaging your child reads every book in the series. The point of early chapter book reading is to practice the skills that your child has developed through Active Reading with you, using a text that they can read on their own. To be sure, with every chapter they finish, they're building that love of reading.

One thing to look for in early chapter books are series, or multiple books that have the same character and often the same format. For example, *The Magic Tree House* mysteries by Mary Pope Osborne follow Jack and Annie through a variety of mysteries. The setting changes (sometimes they're solving a mystery in the time of the dinosaurs and in the next book they're visiting a volcano or the Olympics), but the main characters and structure of the stories is consistent from book to book.

The benefit of series are that children can build background knowledge about the characters—Jack and Annie have the same character traits and approach to solving mysteries in each *Magic Tree House* book—leaving them open to exploring new ideas and building more knowledge. Another benefit is experiencing the connection to reading and characters that adults have. The same way that older readers connect with characters (think *Harry Potter* by J. K. Rowling for tweens, *The Sisterhood of the Traveling Pants* by Ann Brashares for teens, or *The Girl with the Dragon Tattoo* by Stieg Larsson for adults), children can have that experience right from the start with Jack and Annie, Judy Moody, Stink, or any number of characters.

Finally, reading a series helps children by giving them something to read next. This is helpful both to engage children in choosing their own books that you know they can read, and in helping children feel mastery as they read through a series. (A list of chapter books is in Appendix A.)

THE ABCS OF ACTIVE READING CHAPTER BOOKS AND NOVELS

Whether you're reading a chapter book to your child, or encouraging your child to read chapter books on their own, you can do even more with Active Reading as you follow a story from chapter to chapter. When you ask questions, you'll be talking about story grammar across even more action, and helping your child pull the thread of the story through the entire book. You'll be asking questions that help your child develop the visualization skills to imagine the scenes the author has created. Building vocabulary means focusing on words that are important for the story and to support comprehension. And making connections means helping your child connect information that they read earlier in the story to new information the author provides, as well as taking what they know about the fictional world.

Ask Questions

Charlotte's Web by E. B. White is a classic chapter book about a pig (Wilbur) who was born the runt of the litter. He's rescued by Fern who then transfers him to the Zuckermans' farm where Wilbur both learns his fate (to become dinner) and meets his friends, including the spider, Charlotte. Over the course of the book, Charlotte spins elaborate webs that celebrate Wilbur; her efforts end up saving him from being killed. This is a classic children's novel for many reasons, one of which is the amount of conversation that the story can spark.

Two types of questions are important when reading chapter books with your child: story grammar questions and visualizing questions.

Story Grammar Questions

Recall from Chapter 4 that *story grammar* is the structure of stories. As you read to your child, you're already exposing them to a lot of story grammar. Your child knows that stories have settings, characters, and problems and solutions. Chapter books will draw out story grammar into longer, more complex stories, and add some elements like major and minor characters, subplots, and cliff-hangers.

Story questions for chapter books ask about what's happening in the story:

- What happened to the character? Why did that happen?
- What did the character do?
- How did the character feel and why?
- Where did the character go?

All these questions draw your child's attention to the elements of the story and how they change from scene to scene.

For example, reading *Charlotte's Web* by E. B. White to your child, you may ask:

- What kind of pig is Wilbur?
- What happens to Wilbur? What does Wilbur think is going to happen to him?
- What does Charlotte do? How does it help Wilbur?
- Is Templeton the rat nice or not? How do you know? What does Templeton do that is nice or not nice?
- Where do they go? Where is Wilbur in each chapter?

As the story in a chapter book progresses, you'll ask more in-depth and complex questions because your child will know more about the story. At the beginning of a book, you'll ask questions about the characters that are introduced, the setting, and important events (Who is Wilbur? Who is Templeton? Where are they living? What is Wilbur worried about?). As the story evolves, you'll ask about how the characters change (What does Charlotte do and why?), if what the character is doing fits with how the character usually acts or if they are acting "out of character," why a character is doing something (Why does Templeton help Charlotte?), and how the character's actions affect the other characters (What might have happened to Wilbur if Templeton hadn't helped him?). All of these types of questions help children develop a deeper understanding of how to analyze and understand stories.

Reading *Charlotte's Web*, at the start of the story, you'll ask questions like:

- What does Fern want? What would have happened to Wilbur if Fern hadn't rescued him?
- Where does Wilbur go to live?
- Who does Wilbur meet on the Zuckermans' farm?

In the middle of the story, you can ask questions about how the story is progressing and how the characters and their situations are changing:

- What happens to Wilbur when Charlotte writes "Some Pig" in his web?
- Do you think Wilbur likes living on the Zuckermans' farm? Why?
- What do you think will happen to Wilbur when they go to the fair?

At the end of the story, you can ask questions that help bring the story to a conclusion:

- What does Charlotte do for Wilbur? What happens to Wilbur because of Charlotte?
- How does Charlotte feel about Wilbur? How do you know?

For the most part, story questions have answers that are right there in the text. The author will state the answers and there may be pictures to support your child's understanding or they may require a basic inference to answer (e.g., knowing that Wilbur liked the Zuckermans' farm because he got all the food he wanted to eat and had a friend in Charlotte). If your child cannot answer a story question, you can return to the story, reread the part that made you think of the question, and ask again. Or explain to your child how you figured out the answer by telling them the information you used in the book to answer the question.

Visualizing What We Read

Another important part of reading and understanding chapter books, especially as they have fewer and fewer pictures, is *visualization*, or being able to create an image in your mind of what's happening based on the author's words. When we read picture books, the illustrations help us visualize. But, with chapter books and novels with fewer pictures, it requires the reader to create the images themselves.

As they read, children must picture in their head everything from Charlotte's webs spun in the corner of Wilbur's barn stall in *Charlotte's Web* to Charlie floating in a sea of fizzy bubbles in *Charlie and the Chocolate Factory*. Visualizing helps children find the entertainment in what they read—when they can create images in their mind's eye, reading books becomes an interactive experience as they combine the author's words with their own imaginings. You can help your child practice this skill as you read by reading a section, closing the book and either talking about what you see or drawing what you see. Some questions that help your child visualize a story:

- What happened in that part?
- What do you imagine about the setting?
- What do you think that character looks like in that scene?

Build Vocabulary

Chapter books that we read aloud to children often have lots of vocabulary that they do not know, without the illustrations to help them understand it. You don't have to define every new word when reading a chapter book, particularly if that would make it harder for them to follow the actual story. Instead, look for words that are really important for understanding the story and talk about those. This may mean that you stop reading and talk about words and what they mean and you may have to back up and reread portions after defining new words. That's okay.

For example, in *Charlotte's Web*, it's important for a reader to know what a "trough" and "slops" are because some of the book centers on Wilbur liking his slop, and negotiating with Templeton about what he can eat. However, it is less important for them to know what "wheat middlings" and "popovers" are, beyond that they are food that Wilbur eats in his "slop." Knowing what slops in a trough are helps your child visualize Wilbur bellying up to the trough to eat what is basically leftover food. This is enough to move the story along without stopping to define each individual food item.

When you talk about a word, use the same strategy outlined in Chapter 5:

1. Give a child-friendly definition.
2. Connect the word to the story; ask a question about how the word is used in the story.
3. Connect the word to the child's life; talk about how you've used or seen that word in other stories and in life.
4. Use the word outside of reading!

For example, defining the word *runt*, you could:

- Define the word using a child-friendly definition: *A runt is the smallest in a bunch.*
- Connect the word to the story: *Wilbur was the runt of the litter; that means he was the smallest pig in the litter of pigs that was born.*
- Connect to the child's life: *Remember the group of baby kittens we saw? That tiny one is the runt.*

Use the word outside of reading: *Think about other times you see "runts," and times when the word* runt *is not the best way to describe something little, like when you see a little baby.*

Make Connections

There are many ways for your child to connect to chapter books. Three main ones are connecting to background knowledge; connecting from scene to scene; and connecting with characters, events, and feelings.

Make Connections with Background Knowledge

Charlotte's Web takes place on a farm, but your child doesn't have to live on a farm to understand the story. Knowledge about farms from other picture books, a short visit to a farm, and even TV shows can give your child the context to place Wilbur and Charlotte and imagine what's happening on the Zuckermans' farm.

You can build background knowledge about a book by previewing it before you read. Take a look at the back cover, flip through the pages and look for illustrations of characters, and talk about what you think you'll see in the book. This helps your child start to think about what they already know as they start to read.

Some questions to ask to connect your child's knowledge to a new chapter book:

- What do you already know about this setting?
- What do you think about this character?
- Have you read a mystery or funny book before? What do you think you'll like about this book?

Make Connections From Scene to Scene

As your child listens to or reads a chapter book, they are building knowledge about that story. For example, in the first scene in *Charlotte's Web*, we learn that Wilbur is the runt of the litter. This is important throughout the story because it is an important part of his character. His being a runt helps him get saved by Fern, who has compassion for him; it also means that he is not the largest pig at the fair later in the book. Talk about how Wilbur feels being the runt of the litter and what it may make him think about what he can or can't do. Notice that Charlotte never refers to Wilbur's size to describe him in her webs. When reading about the fair, talk about how Wilbur is intimidated by the other, larger pig. All of these connections help your child think about how Wilbur develops throughout the story.

Make Connections with Characters, Events, and Feelings

Making connections with characters, events, and feelings can be as simple as asking your child what they would do if they were in a similar situation. For example, what would they have done if they were in Fern's position and knew that a runt piglet was going to be killed? With chapter books, there are more opportunities to talk about how your child connects with the character, events, and feelings, and how the situation in the story might influence them as well.

Connecting with the elements of a story is one of the main reasons we read—to better understand and relate with people and their lives. Chapter books give us a way to have deeper experiences with characters we love.

RAISING A NOVEL READER

There's nothing better than watching your child diving into a new novel, undaunted by the number of pages, eager to see what's going to happen, and upset when they finish the book because they just didn't want the story to end. As you make this transition in your family's reading time, here are a few things to keep in mind:

- Don't stop reading picture books. Picture books offer rich language, background knowledge, and stories that your child can engage with even as they read chapter books and novels.[1]
- It's okay to put a novel down for a while. If the book hasn't caught your child's attention or they're just not ready for it, put it down and look for something else.
- While you read longer books, allow your child to do something else, like color or play with Legos or draw. When children's hands are busy they can still listen.
- Read just enough. You don't have to read a chapter each time you pick up a book. Reading a few paragraphs or pages of one book may be enough, while you may find yourself reading multiple chapters of another. Your child will progress through each book at its own pace.
- Each time you start reading, review what happened:
  - Where did you leave off with the character?
  - Where were they?
  - What was happening?

ACTIVE READING WITH LONGER STORIES

Reading chapter books with you and on their own is a milestone in a young reader's life. Using the ABCs of Active Reading with chapter books is a way to engage your child in longer, more complex stories that give lots to talk about and connect with, and helps them transition to reading longer chapter books and novels on their own. The next chapter addresses how and why to involve children who struggle with reading in Active Reading.

* * *

WHAT TO REMEMBER

- Children start reading chapter books around age seven or eight when they will start to listen to longer books read aloud, and start reading some chapter books on their own.
- When choosing chapter books to read together, consider:
  - Your child's interests
  - Your child's attention span
  - Your child's background knowledge
  - The type of language in the book, specifically how easy it is for modern children to understand
  - The genre of the book
- To help your child find a book they can read on their own, use the cover and back summary, scan the text, and read the first few pages.
- Ask questions while reading chapter books that help your child understand the story grammar of each chapter and book. You can ask questions about the characters and settings, and the problems and solutions that come up throughout the story. These questions help your child understand and think about how the story develops from scene to scene. Asking questions also helps your child visualize what is happening in a chapter book with fewer pictures to show each scene.
- As the story progresses, you can ask more complex questions as you both know more about the characters and plot.
  - At the start of a story, ask about the initial problems, and the characters that are introduced.
  - In the middle of the story, ask questions about how the characters and story are changing.
  - At the end of the story, ask about how the problem is solved and how the characters feel at the end.
- Chapter books may have more rare words than picture books; you don't have to define every rare word, just enough that your child understands the story and can follow along. Also, you'll want to define words that are most important for understanding the story.
- Three main ways to connect with chapter books include:
  - Making connections to background knowledge
  - Making connections from scene to scene
  - Making connections to characters, events, and feelings

Active Reading and the Struggling Reader

Heather Leavitt knew something was wrong when her son Banks (now a middle-schooler) was in preschool. When it was time to practice letters, Banks would hide under the table. The teachers thought it was a behavior problem, but Leavitt wasn't convinced. Through kindergarten and first grade, Banks had a hard time learning to read and communicate. Even with help from a reading tutor, speech therapist, and occupational therapist, his teachers noted that Banks was "not trying." But Leavitt saw her son putting hours of work into his homework, even as tears streamed down his cheeks. "He was exhausted, and so was I," remembers Leavitt.

At the start of second grade, Leavitt reached outside of their school for testing and learned that Banks had a rare form of dyslexia. He was also gifted, which helped explain how frustrated he was. He'd spent years in school not being able to read, and being very aware of his struggles.

Leavitt sought out a tutor who could provide the type of instruction that Banks needed, and his reading improved rapidly. No longer crying over homework, Banks returned to the carefree, happy child he'd been before school. Looking back on the experience, Leavitt wishes she'd reached out for help earlier. "I still regret not trusting my gut instincts," she recalls.

Throughout the time that Banks struggled, Leavitt read aloud to him. It became a beloved family routine, and a way for Leavitt to share her own love of reading with Banks that she continues today.

Thinking about your child:

- What have you noticed as they learn to read?
- What specific struggles has your child had?
- What do you want reading aloud to provide your child?
- What successes have you already seen with reading or reading aloud?

When Leslie Tennison[1] was reading with her oldest daughter, Ellie, she noticed that even in the fall of first grade, Ellie hadn't had the "lightbulb" moment that Leslie had heard about. She had expected Ellie to have a moment when reading fell into place, and she started picking out words and reading on her own. In particular, Tennison noticed that Ellie wasn't retaining words she read. It was like she read every word for the first time, even simple words like *a* and *the*.

Asking Ellie to sound out words only increased her frustration as she switched *b* for *d*, and misread short words like *slit* as *silt*. Tennison brought the concern to her child's teacher, who started to provide additional support, but Ellie remained aware of her reading struggles, especially as her peers read more and more complex books. At home, Tennison noticed that Ellie rarely initiated reading on her own. She didn't call out street signs or read words in TV ads either. Tennison reads aloud with Ellie, and has noticed that reading aloud is a way for them to build connection and continue to have positive experiences with books even as Ellie struggles with reading basics.

Leavitt's and Tennison's stories are common when it comes to parents of children who struggle to learn to read, and may be familiar to you. Although some struggle when learning to read is common (about ten million children have difficulties learning to read),[2] knowing that it's common doesn't make it easier when you watch your own child struggle. This chapter gives you as a parent the know-how and tools to work with your child's teacher to improve your child's reading and the confidence to know that what you're doing at home will support your child's reading in the long-term.

HOW KIDS CAN STRUGGLE WITH READING

As a parent, you may watch your child struggle to read words. They may, like Banks and Ellie, seem to forget words the second after they read them. You may notice a struggle with reading that was obvious early on—perhaps your child talked later than average, or you noticed they had trouble memorizing letter sounds. Or you may see your child struggle with reading as they learn it in school. Whatever your family's path, knowing some of the core ways that children struggle with reading will help you work with your child's school so you can be an advocate for your child from the start.

When we read on our own, we are combining our ability to read words (also known as *decoding* or *word reading*) with our knowledge of language.[3] If you do not struggle with reading in English, you may experience this when reading in a foreign language—you may be able to decode words and even read quickly, but without the knowledge of the language, you aren't going to understand what you read.

Within reading, there are some aspects of reading that children can struggle with: decoding or word reading, fluency, and comprehension. This section gives an overview, and a starting point to understand children's struggles so that you can use this information to talk with your child's teacher.

Word Reading

Children may struggle to recognize letters and letter sounds and patterns in words, for example, that the letters /oa/ together say /oh/ like boat or goat. When this happens, there are explicit instruction interventions that can quickly teach and reteach sound patterns. Some are provided through schools, and some you can purchase and use on your own (such as *Teach Your Child to Read in 100 Easy Lessons* by Siegfried Engelmann),[4] or your child may benefit from outside tutoring, like Orton-Gillingham or Lindamood-Bell (two options for children with learning differences). If your child is struggling to sound out words, a good next step is to talk with your child's teacher about what in-school interventions can be applied and how you can support your child at home. For example, your child may bring home books with sound patterns they have learned so they can practice word reading at home.

You may notice your child struggling with word decoding as early as pre-school. For example, you may notice that they have a hard time rhyming and aren't able to play word games that ask them to name or change the sounds in words (when rhyming, for instance). For example, if you ask them to name words that start with the same sound as "fish" they may have trouble coming up with "fox," "funny," or other "f" words. If you notice this, talk to your child's school and your pediatrician about next steps you can take.

When your child is older and is reading aloud to you, if you notice your child guessing at words that they should be able to sound out, skipping words when they read aloud, or failing to recall words that occur often in a book (e.g., a name that's repeated), those are other indications that there is a problem. Those signal concerns that your child may not be very good at blending sounds together into a word.

Another important milestone in learning to read is in second grade. At this point, children will encounter longer words that require breaking them apart to sound them out. These are words like compound words (*sandpaper, basketball*), and longer, multisyllabic words (*celebration, invention, unforgettable*). Some children who have done well with reading by memorizing words in first grade will now start to struggle because they don't have the skills to read longer words using what they know about sounds. If at any point you notice your child struggling to read words that you've seen them read before, as Tennison noticed when Ellie was not remembering words she'd sounded out earlier, talk to your child's teacher about how you can work together to support your child.

Questions to ask your child's teacher if you notice a concern with word reading:

- How do you screen students for grade-level word reading skills? And how often are they screened?
- I've noticed a concern with word reading at home; have you seen this at school?
- I'd like for my child to receive some intervention at school for word reading; what kind of intervention do you build into the school day?
  - Who delivers the intervention?
  - What type of instruction is the intervention? Is it a scripted program or a teacher-created intervention?
  - How will you monitor success during the intervention?
  - How long do you deliver an intervention before you assess them for progress?
  - What happens if my child is making progress? What happens if my child does not make progress?
- How will I know what my child is doing and what progress is being made?

Fluency

Reading fluently means reading at a "just right" pace, not too slow and not too fast. When children do not read with fluency, they may read in one- to three-word phrases, not entire sentences. They may sound like robots when they read, with little expression. Or they may read too fast, not stopping for commas and punctuation.

The ultimate goal of fluency is to read at a rate that allows and even supports your understanding of a text. This may be slower than you realize. For example, in second grade (typically fluency is not measured until second-grade reading), children should read at fifty to sixty words per minute at the start of the year, increasing to ninety words per minute by the end of the year.[5] Reading with accuracy and expression is just as important as reading quickly. Reading with accuracy means that you're reading most of the words correctly. And reading with expression means adding emphasis for punctuation, speeding up or slowing down depending on the pace of the story, and even changing voices slightly for various characters that are talking. Expression adds a lot of meaning to reading and influences comprehension.

If you notice your child struggling with fluency at home, you can ask your child's teacher:

- I'm noticing that my child is struggling with reading fluency; have you noticed that?
- What kind of fluency assessments do you give? What do you look for? What is appropriate for my child's grade level?
- Do you think it's a good idea for my child to get an intervention to help with fluency? What instruction in fluency is my child currently getting? What kind of interventions would be helpful?
- How do you monitor progress in fluency? How often do you monitor progress?
- How will I know how my child is doing with fluency?

Comprehension

Comprehension combines word reading and language,[6] so if your child is able to sound out words and read them well, but still is not understanding what they read, they may need to increase their vocabulary or strengthen their language to better understand what they read. That's where Active Reading comes in. Active Reading is not a way to teach word reading, but it can build vocabulary and language comprehension, particularly for struggling readers. In the rest of this chapter, we cover how to build reading comprehension through the ABCs of Active Reading.

WHAT KIDS WHO STRUGGLE WITH READING NEED IN GRADES K–2

Young readers who struggle need two things when they read at home: lots of practice and Active Reading. In many ways, this is exactly what all children need as they learn to read, but parenting a child who struggles may require additional time to practice and more time Active Reading. (Note: Your child's teachers will also create an intervention plan to support your child's reading at school.)

Perfect Practice

Think about any of the skills your child has mastered: riding a bike, playing soccer, dancing ballet. Reading is like those skills. They need to learn how to dance, ride, or read, and then they need lots of opportunities to practice their skills. Of course, they need to be learning the skill in a way that reaches them, as Leavitt found when matching Banks with a reading tutor. Once your child is mastering skills, they need time to practice perfection. It doesn't help them learn to dance if they are not doing the motions correctly. And it doesn't help them learn to read if they are reading the sounds incorrectly. So to learn how to do to something, we must practice perfectly.

The goal of practicing reading is *automaticity*, or recognizing sound patterns and word automatically or without thinking. When kids can read with automaticity, they can focus not on sounding out words but on what the words are saying, essentially listening to what they read from the page.

When your child has a good grasp on word reading, practicing reading also helps them build stamina, or the ability to read longer passages, chapters, and books without stopping. To give your child lots of practice, look for books that are not too hard—that have text that your child can read with accuracy (without help) nine out of ten words (or 90 percent accuracy; more on leveled readers in Chapter 3). A great place to start to find these "just right" books is your child's teacher. Teachers can recommend a set of books that your child can read that may correspond to a letter in a leveled reading set. Once you have a book in hand, have your child read the first page. If you have to give them one out of every ten words they read, that book is too hard (for now).

Using leveled readers is a way to help children practice with texts that they can read mostly on their own. Leveled readers are books that have different "levels" assigned to them. The most common system for organizing reading levels is by letter. So books that are level U are more difficult than level O, and level O books are more difficult than level H. The difficulty comes in whether the book has pictures, the length of the words and sentences, the length of the sentences, and how the text is organized.

Ask your child's teacher what level they are currently working at and get lots of books at that level. You'll probably have a lot of options to choose from. For example, if your child is reading at a level H, you may check out *A Kiss for Little Bear* by Else Minarik, *Danny and the Dinosaur Go to Camp* by Syd Hoff, *I Am Invited to a Party!* by Mo Willems, and *Morris the Moose* by Bernard Wiseman.

To be sure, the leveling system is not perfect and you may have to help your child with more words in one H book than another. They may be able to read *Morris the Moose* independently, but struggle with some of the words in *I Am Invited to a Party!* That's okay. It's also okay to encourage them to read the same book over and over until they are reading it easily. As long as reading is not a chore, they should read and reread as much as they like.

Build Stamina

As your child builds confidence with their sounds and decoding words, it's also important to encourage them to read longer books. Books with longer sentences and stories that take chapters to tell are both good ways to build stamina. It's also important to help your child feel what independent reading feels like.

Reading stamina may require less time than you think. For kindergarten students, by the end of the school year, seven to eight minutes of independent reading is enough time (it may be a struggle for some). For primary grade students, ten to twelve minutes of independent reading should be the goal.

Help your child build stamina by, first, figuring out how long they can read on their own. Once you know (have them read on their own while you time them), set a goal to increase their reading time by a few minutes. Talk about what it looks like when you are reading on your own: they may read out loud to themselves, whisper read, or even read in their head. But the goal is to understand what they are reading. If they get stuck on a word when they are reading by themselves, it's okay to stop and ask for help without stopping reading entirely.

Another way to build reading habits like stamina is to model it. When you can, sit down and read alongside your child so they can see what reading stamina looks like. And after you've read for a set number of minutes or for as long as you want, talk about what you read and what it was like. Do they like reading before bed? After dinner? Was it fun to read outside or do they prefer a favorite reading chair?

When Children Struggle to Make Inferences

One specific struggle that you may notice in your child is in making inferences. Struggling to make inferences, or answer questions that require inferencing is a common concern. Children may have a hard time answering questions, like, What is the character feeling? Or why did he do that? When children struggle to make inferences, it often has to do with how they connect information with what they already know, or how they are connecting information across and within a text, when reading a sentence, paragraph, and story.[7]

If you notice your child has trouble making inferences every time you read—maybe they don't answer questions you think they should be able to—

Tips for Reading with a Struggling Reader

- Take turns reading: You read a page, then your child reads a page to you. You get to hear them read, and they hear you reading fluently throughout the book.
- Choose a character: Books like the *Elephant and Piggie* books by Mo Willems and graphic novels are great for practicing fluency because they are short, often funny, and have pictures that your child can pull from for meaning.
- Get a series: There are many easy reader series books that children can work through. Reading all the *Biscuit* books, *Puppy Mudge* books, or another series gives your child the feeling of accomplishment of reading so many books, and the books become more familiar the more they read.
- Get books that are great for fluency: Books like *You Read to Me, I'll Read to You* by Mary Ann Hoberman and poetry books like *Where the Sidewalk Ends* by Shel Silverstein and *The New Kid on the Block* by Jack Prelutsky are great for practicing fluency.
- Preview words: Before you read, preview or flip through the new book to look at words that you think your child will struggle with. Then read those words outside of the book (write them down or use flashcards) to preview each word before they read it in the story.
- Highlight new sounds and words: Preview a new book and highlight the sound patterns or words your child is working on so they can focus on those words when they come to them.

you can help them improve their ability to make inferences by modeling how to visualize, working at the sentence level by rereading important sentences, using topics that they already know about, and using wordless picture books.

Model How to Visualize

Show your child what you mean when you ask questions that ask them to infer. If your child is not making inferences, they may not know that they are missing information, so showing them how you connect information, even from sentence to sentence, will help them see how to think through connections. For example, remember how greedy Augustus Gloop was in *Charlie and the Chocolate Factory*? And how useless his mother was at stopping his over-the-top eating? As you read *Charlie* with your child, stop and talk about how you envision Augustus and his mother after reading the description in the book. You may even draw out a few scenes to show your child how you're visualizing. Seeing how you create a full picture of Augustus by connecting one piece of information to the next will help your child learn how to construct meaning across sentences.

Reread Important Sections

Particularly if your child is struggling to connect bits of information at the sentence level, reread sections of the story to help them get a literal understanding, then talk about how to connect pieces of information to create a deeper understanding. Rereading is a strategy that your child can use when they are reading on their own to strengthen their comprehension and build meaning.

Work at the Sentence Level

If your child is having a hard time making inferences about chapters or sections of a story, narrow the scope to the sentence level. In *Dory Fantasmagory* by Abby Hanlon, Dory refuses to get dressed to go to the doctor's because she is pretending to be a dog. Instead of talking about how Dory's mother feels across the whole chapter, during which she becomes increasingly frustrated with Dory, you can ask, "How does her mother feel about what Dory is doing right now?" Then talk about that at the sentence level, looking at what her mother says and connecting it with a time when your child was dawdling (in this case, fortunately, adult reactions to kids' dawdling are fairly universal).

Build a Bridge

As you help your child make inferences, draw from what they already know or have experienced. This can be as simple and pointing out that they've had an experience like Alexander in *Alexander and the Terrible, Horrible, No Good, Very Bad Day* by Judith Viorst and can use that to better understand the story.

Use Wordless Picture Books

Wordless picture books, like *Journey, Quest,* and *Return* by Aaron Becker, provide opportunities to practice inferencing without using text. Have the same conversation that you would have with a book with text, and point out to your child what they are doing as they infer (find more book recommendations in Appendix A). This helps children realize that they have the skills to think critically about text, once they get the information off the page, as it were.

Active Reading with Struggling Readers

Leavitt and her children, Banks and his younger sister, who also has dyslexia, spend time reading aloud together every night. Even though both kids are now in middle school, reading aloud is still a favorite nighttime ritual and one that often runs overtime. Sometimes they talk before they read; other times they dive into the story. They read until they can leave the character at a good place, because, says Leavitt, "we have a rule that we don't want to leave the character in a bad spot before we stop for the night."

Reading aloud has helped Leavitt share her love of reading and build a closeness between her and her children. It's also expanded her kids' vocabulary and prepared them to be successful as readers, even as they struggle to decipher text word by word. By now, it comes as no surprise that Active Reading is something that helps struggling readers. Specifically, as Leavitt has found, it helps them build their listening skills, and their language and vocabulary, both of which contribute to comprehension.

Listening may not seem like it connects to reading, but when we read words, we hear them in our mind. In that way, listening comprehension, or a child's ability to understand what is said (or read aloud) to them is an important aspect of reading comprehension. For children who struggle to learn to read, the relationship between reading and listening comprehension increases in importance as children move through school.[8] Therefore, as children gain reading skill, they use their listening comprehension more and more to understand what they are reading on their own.

Active Reading can provide children who struggle with reading a stronger vocabulary,[9] which is an important part of reading comprehension. Children who are struggling with reading for any number of reasons have also benefited from reading aloud. In one study, children who were at-risk practiced Active Reading scored higher than other students on a narrative retell (retelling stories) and on vocabulary learning.[10]

As Tennison and Leavitt found when reading aloud with their kids, reading aloud is a way to keep children who are struggling with reading connected to books and immersed in positive reading experiences. Active Reading, when you are doing all the "work" of reading words and reading with fluency, can maintain your child's interest in books, especially because you are exposing them to books that are at a higher level than they can read on their own. Leavitt has also found that reading popular books with her kids (right now they're deep into *Harry Potter*) helps them socially. They can keep up with their friends and talk about the latest popular stories. Reading aloud expands their access to books far beyond their comfortable reading level.

The nice thing about reading with your child is that Active Reading looks the same with children who are doing well with reading and those who are struggling. The ABCs still apply and the conversation may look very much the same (see Chapters 4–7). Active Reading can be a time in your day when books are the focus, but there is no struggle.

MORE WAYS TO SUPPORT A CHILD
WHO STRUGGLES WITH READING

Remember that your child is doing the best they can; your job is to work with your child's teachers, and to make your child feel good about their progress and how they can engage with books. Active Reading can be a way to keep the fun in reading for your child as you work on improving their word reading, fluency, and vocabulary.

Here are more ways to support your struggling reader:

- Notice and celebrate your child's strengths. Notice when you see them excel at something that is not reading and encourage them to explore their interests.
- Be realistic with your goals. Reading is a process, and it takes time and years of practice to learn to do well. Your child has all the way through grade 12 to practice and get better. At home, you may set the goal of reading aloud to each other for ten minutes each night, or to read level H books by the end of the year. Setting smaller goals teaches your child that they can make progress and show them how their hard work is paying off.
- Don't shy away from reading complex books to your child, even if they struggle with reading.[11] Children who struggle with reading can engage and learn from complex picture books. In fact, children who struggled with reading and were engaged in reading aloud performed higher on language assessments than children who had not been read to.[12]

A reading concern in one grade, or during one phase of learning to read, also does not mean that your child will struggle with reading forever or that they will not enjoy school or learning. Reading is a complex process that takes time.

RAISING ACTIVE READERS

Many children struggle to learn to read. Whatever your child's struggles are (word reading, fluency, or comprehension), Active Reading can provide a way to keep your child interested and connected with reading, and strengthen their language skills and vocabulary along the way. Now that we've covered the ABCs of Active Reading, using picture books, nonfiction, chapter books, and novels, the final step is to make your child into a lifelong Active Reader.

* * *

WHAT TO REMEMBER

- When children struggle with reading, they may struggle with word reading, fluency, and comprehension.
- Struggling readers need lots of practice reading (mostly) perfectly, meaning that they are reading the words correctly and fixing mistakes quickly.
- Leveled readers are a way for struggling readers to work with books that are just right for them, right now.
- Children should also focus on building stamina, or the ability to read for longer periods of time. Kindergarteners may only read for a short burst (seven to eight minutes), and they will build up to ten and then twenty minutes from there.
- If your child struggles to make inferences, model it, reread important sections, make inferences at the sentence level, build a bridge from what they know to new information, or use wordless picture books to help them practice inferring.
- During Active Reading, ask your child questions that encourage them to infer (usually starting with *Why* or *How*). Then encourage them to talk more about their thinking with questions like, What in the story made you think that? How do you know? It will take many conversations for your child to learn how to infer and to make it a habit during their own reading.
- Active Reading helps children who struggle with reading build comprehension of what they read on their own by improving their listening comprehension and vocabulary. Listening comprehension is a child's ability to understand what is said or read aloud to them. As children gain reading skill, they use their listening comprehension more and more to understand what they read.

10

Raising an Active Reader

Reading *Belle the Birthday Fairy*, one of the many *Rainbow Magic* books by Daisy Meadows, Sarah, age six, listens to the story unfold: the two main characters, Kirsty and Rachel, are planning a surprise party for Rachel's mother.

"What is a surprise party?" Sarah asks, interrupting her mom.

"It's when you plan a birthday party for someone and they don't know that you're planning it," her mother explains.

They keep reading. Sarah stops her mom to inquire about words she doesn't know, *astonishment* and *unlucky*. Sarah refers back to the map at the start of the book to figure out where the girls are at the start of the story. She wonders when the girls will find the birthday fairy, and they talk about the problem that the fairies have to solve: the birthday party planning that has gone disastrously wrong.

All this conversation is helping Sarah become an Active Reader, and she's taken the lead asking questions, building her own vocabulary, and making connections from the map to the story, and from the other Rainbow Fairy books she's read to this one. That's the goal: that our kids listen and engage with us when we are reading with them and learn how to engage with books on their own.

Thinking about how you have engaged your child in Active Reading:

- What Active Reading habits have they picked up?
  - Are they asking questions more?
  - Are they talking and thinking about words they don't know?

○ Are they seeing more connections between what they've read and what they know?

As you read with your child, look for those Active Reading strategies that they are bringing into their own life and encourage them to become Active Readers in their own right.

At this point, you know that Active Reading is the goal not only for us but also for our kids. When kids are able to think critically as they read, when they ask questions, think about and learn new words, and make connections, they are becoming strong readers.

The best way to raise an Active Reader is to make it a (fun) habit. First and foremost, Active Reading should be a fun thing that you and your child engage in at least a few times a week, if not every night. Ideally, we'd read with our children every day, but realizing that life gets busy and fast, and sometimes other activities (or bedtime) becomes more pressing than reading, setting a goal of reading with your child at least three times a week for fifteen minutes each time may be enough. And you may find yourself reading past bedtime as you read just one more scene or keep going until your character is not in peril.

In this chapter, we finish with how to help your child become an Active Reader by keeping Active Reading a regular practice, taking the ABCs beyond books, helping them find topics they're interested in, and keeping reading aloud alive in your family.

ACTIVE READERS BEYOND THIRD GRADE

We've already talked about how reading is a combination of getting the words off the page (e.g., sounding out words) and language.[1] In the early elementary school years, children are learning the basic mechanics of reading, as well as how to think about what they read. As they age, reading skills will become less about discrete skills (sounding out words) and more about broader thinking skills. As the books get more challenging, from third grade to middle school and into high school, how children interact with text and what they are expected to do on their own will also get more complex.

In the upper grades, children will spend approximately 85 percent of their day on assignments that require reading and working with a text.[2] Beyond early elementary school, the ability to use metacognition, or the ability to think while they read, differentiates strong readers from those who struggle to get meaning from what they read. Readers who have strong metacognition are able to have a conversation with themselves while they read, and this helps them comprehend and connect with text.

A metacognitive reader is able to preview text in a way that helps them understand and get interested in what they're about to read. This could mean that they flip through a nonfiction book and think about what they already know about the topic and what they want to learn, like the book walk described in Chapter 7. Or it could mean that they read the first few pages of a novel and are already making connections with the characters, forming predictions about what could happen, and wondering what will happen next, as they connect with stories (see Chapters 6 and 8).

As they read, readers with metacognitive skills will engage in a dialogue with themselves. Essentially, they'll have the type of Active Reading conversation with the text, in their minds, that you've had with them out loud. They're thinking about questions (What is the most important part of this story? What should I be learning about this topic?). They're creating images in their head about what's happening or what the author is explaining. They're identifying words they don't know and defining them before they move on. When they put a book down, they're summarizing what they learned before they start reading again. And they're making connections with everything from their background knowledge about nonfiction topics, to what they know about character archetypes or story structure, as they read to gain even more meaning. To be sure, the ABCs of Active Reading are something that your child will take with them through school and into adulthood.

KEEP YOUR CHILD READING

It can seem easier to engage your child in books when they're younger. At that point, you're in control of bedtime and can incorporate reading into their bedtime routine. As they grow and take more control of their time and interests, you can keep books front and center by making them special and keeping the conversation going about what they're reading, even when you're not reading the book together.

- Keep "selling" books to them. Make books a special part of their day—with their own library that they can keep in their bedroom (which could be as small as a shelf full of books), weekly trips to the library, and creating wish lists of books for birthdays and holidays. These are all ways to keep books a special part of their experience that they'll look forward to.

- Read a series. Book series are a great way to keep developing readers engaged, but series are also ways to keep older children interested. Series like the *Percy Jackson* books by Rick Riordan, and the *Time Quintet* series by Madeleine L'Engle, and whatever new novels are popular at school. When they're finished with one series, look for books that are similar by asking a teacher or librarian, or even doing an internet search: If you like this book, what should you read next?
- Find different purposes for reading. As your child grows, how they use texts can develop too. Find ways for your child to contribute to the household, or develop new skills through reading. For example, can they read travel books to plan the next family vacation? Or could they figure out the best way to solve a problem using a how-to book?

Take advantage of the ways that your child can access books and reading to expand and engage them with anything and everything. That not only keeps them reading, but it also shows them how reading can be helpful across their lives.

TAKING THE ABCS OF ACTIVE READING BEYOND BOOKS

The thinking that your child can do because of the Active Reading you do together is not just for books. You can ask questions about documentaries you watch or things you observe in your backyard. You can build vocabulary about a specific topic they're interested in, from woodworking in the garage to gardening to sewing. You can build background knowledge by talking about what you know, or about what they learn through their own interests and connect that to what they've observed or already know. All this develops critical thinking, curiosity, and important skills that help them be engaged with their world.

Ask Questions

- **Ask open-ended questions.** When your child notices something, or you're exploring anything from a museum exhibit to the beach, ask open-ended questions:
  - What do you notice?
  - What do you think about that?
  - What could have caused that to happen?
  - What do you think will happen next?
- **Generate new questions to explore.** For example, during a trip to an amusement park, your child may wonder, What makes roller coasters move? How do roller coasters not fall off the track when they go upside

down? How fast do roller coasters go? You can write these questions down, even on a scrap of paper, and try to find the answers using a combination of books, online resources, and videos when you get home. The point is not to answer every question in detail, but to go through the process of exploring a topic and generating questions along the way.

- **Don't ask "How was school today?"** Instead of asking your child about the specifics of their day (and what child really gives a full answer anyway?) ask what new things they learned at school or what was surprising to them. Then try to generate conversation based off of your child's answer. Some more creative questions include:
  - What is a compliment you would give yourself today?
  - What was the most interesting thing you learned or saw today?
  - What was the silliest thing you saw today? What made you laugh?
  - What were you grateful for today?
  - What would your best friend say about today?
  - If you could go back, what would you change about today?
  - What made you feel most happy, satisfied, or excited today?

Build Vocabulary

Words are all around us, and the most important words to your child may not be in a book. They may wonder how to find the exact words to describe a situation that happened to them, they may want to name all the bugs they collected from your yard, or they may want to use the right words in their school essay. Whatever their reason, you can build your child's vocabulary with the following techniques:

- **Notice new words.** Define words you come across in conversation or in the environment. Your child may see new words on billboards, hear them on the radio, or notice them in advertisements. When you come across a new word, define it on the spot, including using a dictionary (online or paper) to get a firm definition.
- **Get specific.** When you're talking with your child or helping them with homework, ask them to think about the most specific word they can use to describe something. Was the day "great," or can they think of a more specific word (*stupendous, amazing, fantastic*)?

Make Connections

We're building background knowledge all the time. Taking the time to talk about what's happening in your child's day-to-day experiences is a great way to build that background knowledge and maintain a connection as your child gets older.

- **Talk about everyday experiences.** Use what happens around your house every day as conversation. When your child is younger, this may look like talking through errands and talking about what they notice. As your child gets older, it'll be about situations they're experiencing in their friendships or relationships and problems they see in their community and world.
- **Make use of community resources.** Libraries, museums, local festivals, and more are great experiences to build background knowledge. You don't have to spend lots of money or even go far from home to have a range of experiences that your child can draw from.
- **Follow your child's interests.** If your child has an interest in anything from baking to mechanics, ask around to see how you can help develop it. Could a local bakery host a tour? Could your child spend an hour "working" alongside a local mechanic? Look for the experts in your area that could encourage your child's interests with some hands-on practice.
- **Listen.** In all the conversation, try to do more listening than talking. Asking open-ended questions and helping your child make connections lead them to talking and thinking out loud. Then you get to listen and respond, shaping their thinking along the way.

DEVELOP YOUR CHILD'S INTERESTS AND PASSIONS

Finding your child's passions can feel like a daunting task (they try everything), or it may be completely obvious (they've only ever wanted to play soccer, read about soccer, talk about soccer). From an Active Reading standpoint, finding your child's passions can help guide what they read about as well as what they explore outside of reading. Either way, helping your child find what they are good at, and then expanding on their talent and interests is one of the most rewarding parts of parenting.

- **Nurture natural talents.** If your child has a talent that emerges early— an interest in dance and performance, a talent for art or a sport—nurture it. Even if your child doesn't pursue that specific talent—say they have an early interest in soccer but then decide they don't want to be on the soccer team after all—it may manifest itself another way. Perhaps they are great at being a team leader or have an interest in sports medicine.

- **Encourage your child to develop knowledge about their interests.** Knowing the ins and outs of a topic—soccer, horses, swimming—turns the interest from something that they do to something that they can be an expert on.
- **Use homework as a springboard.** For older children, help them see how their strengths in school can carry over into other areas. A talent in math or science may help them think through problem solving in other areas. Or if you notice that your child loves to solve problems, help them carry that into other areas of their life. Taking some of the skills that your child is using in school to out-of-school settings can help your child see the benefit, and broaden their understanding of how the world works.
- **Talk about their interests.** Keep the conversation going about what they're interested in:
  ○ What are they wondering?
  ○ What do they want to learn next?
  ○ What do they want to know about or experience?
- **Don't forget help around the house.** Giving your child chores can also shed light on what they are good at. You may notice that your child is great at organizing small piles of things, but not as good at tackling larger projects (cleaning a very messy room). Noticing this can help you see how your child may tackle other types of projects.
- **Get bored.** Being bored is okay. Being bored, or not having something structured to do, can improve kids' creativity.[3] It also helps kids find their motivation and feel what it's like to be self-motivated.[4] Both of these—being forced to get creative with their time and figuring out how to start something new—are great for helping children find what motivates them and how they want to spend their time.

KEEPING READING ALOUD ALIVE IN YOUR FAMILY

At this point, hopefully reading with your child is a habit that you enjoy and a family tradition that you want to keep building. It's something your children expect and something that you've incorporated into your daily life at home. But with every shift in your children's development, you'll make changes in the schedule, like the change from summer to back to school, the shift from one grade to the next, and the important change from your child reading with help to reading entirely on their own. All of these will change the purpose of reading aloud in your house. Active Reading will change too. You'll go from reading lots of picture books that inspire lots of questions to reading novels where you may not stop reading for pages before finding a scene or word to talk about. The important thing is to keep reading!

You may set a family goal around reading aloud. Perhaps you want to read all the *Harry Potter* books (no small task!). Maybe you want to read five novels over the course of the year. Perhaps you want to read five novels from five different countries. Or you want to read aloud together every day for a year. These goals can keep you motivated when it's going well (when everybody loves the book) and when it's not (when only one person loves the book).

Let your children choose the books. As they get older, look for books that they can't read on their own yet. Look for books that are just out of their range in terms of word reading, but that they can understand when read aloud. For elementary schoolers, this may be *The Hobbit* by J. R. R. Tolkien or some books by Roald Dahl. For upper elementary schoolers, it may be the historical novel *Chains* by Laurie Halse Anderson. When choosing a text, however, keep the content in mind. Some books that are technically a few grade levels above are about topics that are too violent or inappropriate for younger children.

Read popular books. Some books are wonderful just to share, regardless of reading level or the fact that your child can read them on their own. Reading *Wonder* by R. J. Palacio may provide a good bonding experience, or sharing *Misty of Chincoteague* by Marguerite Henry may be the perfect way to share your child's love of horses.

However your approach reading aloud in your family, communicate that it's important. Rearrange other things you do during the day—cut short screen time, even limit homework time—to get in those fifteen minutes of reading aloud each night. We know it's worth it!

Appendix A

Book Lists

The book lists in this appendix are meant to help you identify books that can start or extend your Active Reading journey. This is not an exhaustive list, and new books are always being published. Two great resources to find more books are at your local library and Brightly (www.readbrightly.com). You can also find book ideas through annual awards like the Caldecott Medal lists (www.ala.org) and others.

PICTURE BOOKS

Each of these picture books has detailed illustrations, complex stories, and rich vocabulary. These are books that provide a lot to talk about and stories that are worth sharing with children in grades K–3.

Picture Book Authors

These authors have published lots of books that are great for Active Reading with kids in grades K–3.

Chris van Allsburg's picture books (*The Stranger*, *Two Bad Ants*, *Jumanji*, *The Garden of Abdul Gasazi*, and *Zathura*) are imaginative and sometimes dark stories.

Jan Brett's stories (*The Mitten*, *Gingerbread Baby*, *Armadillo Rodeo*) are fun books to read and have highly detailed illustrations.

Janell Cannon (*Stellaluna*, *Verdi*, *Pinduli*, and *Crickwing*) writes books with animals as main characters that are imaginative and descriptive.

Matt de la Peña (*Carmela Full of Wishes*, *Last Stop on Market Street*) is a contemporary author who tells stories that capture different snippets of everyday life.

Tony DiTerlizzi is the author of *Ted* and the illustrator of *The Spider and the Fly* (authored by Mary Howitt), both fun books to read that have rich, detailed illustrations.

Kevin Henkes has written many books that resonate with the early elementary school experience, from *Sheila Rae, the Brave* to *Wemberly Worried.*

Russell Hoban wrote the *Frances* books (*Bedtime for Frances, A Birthday for Frances, A Bargain for Frances*). *Frances* stories are about familiar topics for children, told through the antics of Frances the badger.

Patricia Polacco has written picture books that appeal to second and third graders on topics including community and family (*Holes in the Sky*) to finding your talents (*The Junkyard Wonders*) and the *Titanic* (*The Bravest Man in the World*).

William Steig (*Brave Irene, Sylvester and the Magic Pebble*) is another classic picture book author. Kids love the imagination and whimsy in his stories.

Judith Viorst (*Alexander and the Terrible, Horrible, No Good, Very Bad Day* and *Alexander, Who Used to Be Rich Last Sunday*) tells stories about real-life experiences with humor that kids and adults will appreciate.

Bernard Waber writes stories about common childhood experiences, like *Ira Sleeps Over*, as well as books about an over-the-top family pet in the *Lyle, Lyle, Crocodile* books.

Vera B. Williams (*A Chair for My Mother, Cherries and Cherry Pits*) does a wonderful job of telling stories that show the strength of family.

Picture Books

These picture books have wonderful stories that your child will remember long after they are reading on their own.

An anthology like *The 20th Century Children's Book Treasury* by Janet Schulman puts lots of classic stories all between two covers. Your child may return to this treasury for stories like *Where the Wild Things Are* by Maurice Sendak, *Madeline* by Ludwig Bemelmans, and *The Snowy Day* by Ezra Jack Keats.

Miss Rumphius by Barbara Cooney tells the story of a lady who has promised to make the world more beautiful, and how she goes about doing that.

Jabari Jumps by Gaia Cornwall is the story of Jabari's first time jumping off the high dive, and a story to help any child tackle something new and a little bit scary.

Carmela Full of Wishes by Matt de la Peña is about a little girl who joins her brother while running errands and learns about her neighborhood. She finds a dandelion and has to decide which wish to make.

The Last Stop on Market Street by Matt de la Peña is the story of CJ and his grandmother taking their weekly trip to the soup kitchen, and all the experiences they have along the way.

Alfie: The Turtle That Disappeared by Thyra Heder alternates perspective between a girl, Nia, and her pet turtle, when he disappears on her seventh birthday. It's a good book to use to talk about point of view and who is telling the story.

Hey, Little Ant by Phillip Hoose shows children about perspective with a story about how an ant feels when you're about to step on him.

The Story of Ferdinand by Munro Leaf is about a bull who would rather sit and smell the flowers than fight, and about being yourself, no matter what.

Roxaboxen by Alice McLerran tells the story of a village created by a group of children. This is a great example of a story where the setting takes center stage, not the characters.

A Chair for My Mother by Vera B. Williams is the story of how one little girl saves up to buy her mother a comfortable chair so she can relax after work. It's about the importance of thinking of others.

Because by Mo Willems shows how a little inspiration has a big effect.

Wordless Picture Books

Wordless picture books are a great way to get kids talking about books. You can use the pictures to make inferences, talk about story structure, and generally wonder about the story. These wordless picture books are good for kids in elementary school.

Quest, Return, and *Journey* by Aaron Becker
Castle, Cathedral, and *City* by David Macauley
The Lion and the Mouse and *The Tortoise and the Hare* by Jerry Pinkney
Another by Christian Robinson
Tuesday, Flotsam, Sector 7 and others by David Wiesner
Chalk and *Fossil* by Bill Thomson

Books about Words and Love of Language

The Word Collector by Peter Reynolds tells the story of Jerome, who collects words all around him. Kids will learn about the different kinds of words and talk about how they can categorize the words they hear.

The Boy Who Loved Words by Roni Schotter is the story of a boy who collects words and finds a way to share them.

Seeds and Trees: A Children's Book about the Power of Words by Brandon Walden explores the power of words on feelings.

The Word Collector by Sonja Wimmer is the story of a girl who loves words told in a poem.

Picture Books about Topics Kids Want to Talk About

Picture books provide an opening for conversation about lots of topics that are important to kids, and that can be difficult to explain, like death, moving, and inclusion.

Death

Where Do They Go? by Julia Alvarez is a poem-like book that can start a conversation about what it feels like to remember someone who has passed away.

Ida, Always by Caron Lewis tells the story of two polar bears in Central Park Zoo and what happens when one of them dies.

The Rough Patch by Brian Lies is the story of what happens when a fox loses his dog and best companion.

The Remember Balloons by Jessie Oliveros uses the metaphor of balloons to represent the memories we have.

The Tenth Good Thing about Barney by Judith Viorst is about how a little boy deals with the death of his cat.

Moving

Dreamers by Yuyi Morales is a big-picture story about moving and about immigration, tracking the story of a mother and child traveling together, and how they find a space that inspires them.

Lenny and Lucy by Philip Stead shows how one child solves the problem of feeling like a new house is not welcoming.

Double Happiness by Nancy Tupper Ling tells a story in poems of moving from one home to another.

Florette by Anna Walker explores how Mae brings what she loved about her old home—the garden, apple trees, and butterflies—to her new home in the city.

Inclusion

The Big Umbrella by Amy June Bates and Juniper Bates turns the idea of kindness and being inclusive into the metaphor of an umbrella.

The Snurtch by Sean Ferrell explores how one little girl's negative actions affect her peers.

Stick and Stone by Beth Ferry takes a humorous look at how we can stick up for each other.

Dealing with Negative Feelings

Chester's Way by Kevin Henkes is a story of how we can change and get out of our habits when a new friend comes along.

Grumpy Monkey by Suzanne Lang is a funny book about a monkey who has to deal with everyone else trying to get him out of a bad day.

Strictly No Elephants by Lisa Mantchev is the story of a unique pet club, where everyone is included.

The Adventures of Beekle: The Unimaginary Friend by Dan Santat is the story of how one imaginary friend came to be, and a great jumping-off point to talk about how we meet our friends, real and imaginary.

The Other Side by Jacqueline Woodson tells the story of two girls who make friends despite a fence that divides their neighborhoods, one White, one African American.

Alexander and the Terrible, Horrible, No Good, Very Bad Day by Judith Viorst is a classic tale of one boy's bad day, and learning that bad days happen to everyone.

Being Yourself, No Matter What

Mr. Tiger Goes Wild by Peter Brown is the story of a tiger who wants to be more wild, and how his more civilized animal friends respond.

Stand Tall, Molly Lou Melon by Patty Lovell is a story about friendship that celebrates being yourself, even when someone teases you.

Ish by Peter Reynolds tells the story of Ramon, an artist who learns to appreciate his "ish" art that isn't perfect but is meaningful.

Gender Identity

Red: A Crayon's Story by Michael Hall explores what happens to Red, a crayon that actually draws in blue.

I Am Jazz by Jessica Herthel and Jazz Jennings is the true life story of Jazz Jennings, a spokesperson for transgender children.

Jacob's New Dress by Sarah Hoffman tells the story of what happens when a little boy wants to wear a dress to school.

BunnyBear by Andrea Loney explores a bear that identifies with bunnies and can't, until he meets Grizzlybun.

Julián Is a Mermaid by Jessica Love is the story of a little boy who wants to dress up as a mermaid and how his grandmother encourages him.

Accepting Your Name

Chrysanthemum by Kevin Henkes tells the story of a little mouse that loves her name, until she starts school.

The Name Jar by Yangsook Choi tells the story of Unhei, who moved from Korea and is frustrated when she finds that her classmates struggle to pronounce her name. She tries to take on other, American, names, but in the end chooses her original Korean one.

Phoebe Sounds It Out by Julie Zwillich is about a girl whose name doesn't look like it sounds and the funny, endearing story that results as she tries to reconcile her name with its spelling.

Stories about Kindness and Friendship at School

The Invisible Boy by Trudy Ludwig is about a boy that no one notices, until a new kid comes to school.

Thank You, Mr. Falker by Patricia Polacco is the story of a girl who has dyslexia and a teacher who will not give up on her.

Officer Buckle and Gloria by Peggy Rathmann is about a friendship between a safety officer and his dog.

The Smallest Girl in the Smallest Grade by Justin Roberts is about a girl who isn't noticed by her peers, but who notices everything around her, including standing up to bullies.

Take Your Octopus to School Day by Audrey Vernick is about friendship and building friends in school around shared interests.

Each Kindness by Jacqueline Woodson is a story about bullying and being the new girl in school.

Family

Islandborn by Junot Diaz is a story about Lola as she develops her understanding of her family through a school project. It's a wonderful book to talk about how people come to the United States, and your own family history.

Wolfie the Bunny by Ame Dyckman discusses the topics of getting a new sibling and adoption.

Julius, the Baby of the World by Kevin Henkes is a classic picture book about jealousy over a new sibling.

The Keeping Quilt by Patricia Polacco traces the story of a family through an heirloom quilt.

Picture Books about Science, Technology, Engineering, and Math (STEM) Topics

Andrea Beaty's picture books *Ada Twist, Scientist*, *Rosie Revere, Engineer*, *Iggy Peck, Architect*, and *Sofia Valdez, Future Prez* explain the thinking and processes that go into various jobs, and are told in a fun, rhyming cadence.

Cece Loves Science and *Cece Loves Science and Adventure* by Kimberly Derting are about Cece, a budding scientist who uses STEM skills to solve problems and do experiments.

Everything You Need for a Treehouse by Carter Higgins is a story with lots of detailed illustrations that you can use to talk about how we create spaces.

Stuck by Oliver Jeffers tells the story of what happens after a boy gets a kite stuck in a tree. A great book to talk about problem solving and how we may throw everything at a problem without solving it.

Funny Picture Books

These books are great when you want a lighthearted read, and you never know what your child will connect with!

The Day the Crayons Quit and *The Day the Crayons Came Home* by Drew Daywalt are stories about crayons that have had enough, told using an interesting storytelling format and lots of humor.

The Good Egg and *The Bad Seed* by Jory John tell the stories of what really happens to these idioms.

Click, Clack, Moo: Cows That Type by Doreen Cronin, and other books with Farmer Brown, Duck, and the cows by Cronin, are about animals that run Farmer Brown's farm.

Amelia Bedelia by Peggy Parish. This book series (there are the original *Amelia Bedelia* and many easy readers) has lots of idioms and expressions that your child may need to talk through.

Dragons Love Tacos and *Dragons Love Tacos 2* by Adam Rubin are about, well, dragons and tacos (and a time machine).

After the Fall by Dan Santat takes the story of Humpty Dumpty past the fall.

The True Story of the 3 Little Pigs by Jon Scieszka tells the Three Little Pigs from the wolf's perspective.

The Stinky Cheese Man and Other Fairly Stupid Tales by Jon Scieszka has lots of fairy tales that are turned on their heads.

Fairy Tales and Other Classic Picture Book Stories

These books will introduce your child to the big stories in our world, including folktales, fairy tales, and other classic stories.

Cynthia Rylant is the author of fairy-tale retellings for many classic tales, including *Cinderella, Hansel and Gretel, Beauty and the Beast*, and *Sleeping Beauty*.

Rachel Isadora has retold fairy tales like *The Princess and the Pea, Rapunzel, Hansel and Gretel*, and others using rich artwork that reflects diverse cultures.

Multicultural Fairy Tales

The Korean Cinderella by Shirley Climo
The Rough-Face Girl by Rafe Martin
La Princesa and the Pea by Susan Middleton Elya
The Orphan: A Cinderella Story from Greece by Anthony Manna
Rapunzel by Chloe Perkins
The Ghanaian Goldilocks by Dr. Tamara Pizzoli
Cendrillon: A Caribbean Cinderella by Robert San Souci
Lon Po Po: A Red Riding Hood Story from China by Ed Young

Myths

A Child's Introduction to Greek Mythology: The Stories of the Gods, Goddesses, Heroes, Monsters, and Other Mythical Creatures by Heather Alexander

Greek Myths for Young Children by Heather Amery
King Midas and the Golden Touch by Charlotte Craft
Pegasus by Marianna Mayer

Folktales and Other Stories

Anansi the Spider: A Tale from the Ashanti by Gerald McDermott
Why Mosquitos Buzz in People's Ears by Verna Aardema
Stone Soup by Marcia Brown
The Classic Treasury of Aesop Fables by Don Daily
Strega Nona by Tomie dePaola
Why the Sky Is Far Away by Mary-Joan Gerson
The Girl Who Loved Wild Horses by Paul Goble
Just So Stories by Rudyard Kipling
Fables by Arnold Lobel
Zomo the Rabbit: A Trickster Tale from Africa by Gerald McDermott
The Talking Eggs by Robert San Souci
Mufaro's Beautiful Daughters by John Steptoe

CHAPTER BOOKS TO READ ALOUD

Illustrated Chapter Books

These chapter books are great to read aloud with your child because they have enough illustration to support the text, and are a good introduction to chapter books.

James and the Giant Peach by Roald Dahl
Charlie and the Chocolate Factory by Roald Dahl
Fantastic Mr. Fox by Roald Dahl
Charlotte's Web by E. B. White
Stuart Little by E. B. White

Illustrated Chapter Book Series

Anna Hibiscus series by Atinuke (*Anna Hibiscus, You're Amazing, Anna Hibiscus!* and *Hooray for Anna Hibiscus!*). This series is about a little girl who lives in Africa with her family, including a mother from Canada, her African father, and her grandparents, aunties, and uncles. This is a great book series to show what life is like in another place.
Zoey and Sassafras by Asia Citro (*Dragons and Marshmallows, Monsters and Mold, Unicorns and Germs, The Pod and the Bog*). In each story, Zoey and her cat Sas-

safras come across a magical creature and a problem that has to be solved using science.

The *Mercy Watson* series by Kate DiCamillo (*Mercy Watson to the Rescue, Mercy Watson Goes for a Ride, Mercy Watson Fights Crime,* and *Mercy Watson: Princess in Disguise*) Mercy is a pig that gets into all kinds of antics while trying to find one thing: hot buttered toast.

The *Mango and Bambang* books by Polly Faber are the witty, funny stories about Mango Allsorts, a girl who's good at lots of things, and her pet not-a-pig Tapir.

The Princess in Black series by Shannon Hale (*The Science Fair Scare, The Perfect Princess Party, The Hungry Bunny Horde, The Mysterious Playdate*). The Princess in Black (or Princess Magnolia) is a princess, until she's needed to stop monsters from eating goats. Can she keep her secret identity a secret from the Duchesses, goat herders, and other princesses?

Dory Fantasmagory by Abby Hanlon (*The Real True Friend, Head in the Clouds, Dory Dory Black Sheep,* and *Tiny Tough*). Dory, the youngest in her family, has two older siblings who don't pay her as much attention as she'd like, and an imaginary world with friends, a fairy godmother, and a villain to keep her busy.

Toys Go Out by Emily Jenkins are the stories of three toys—a plush stingray, a toy buffalo, and a plastic ball—and their adventures.

Lulu and the Duck in the Park and other *Lulu* books by Hilary McKay are stories about a little girl and her adventures with animals.

NOVELS

These books make great read-alouds when your child doesn't need pictures to support their understanding and can listen to longer, more complex stories, creating images in their minds as you read.

Mr. Popper's Penguins by Richard Atwater

The Penderwicks series by Jeanne Birdsall

The Secret Garden by Frances Hodgson Burnett

The *Ramona* books by Beverly Cleary (*Ramona Quimby, Age 8, Beezus and Ramona, Ramona the Pest, Ramona the Brave*)

The *Ralph S. Mouse* collection by Beverly Cleary (*Ralph S. Mouse, The Mouse and the Motorcycle, Runaway Ralph*)

Books by Roald Dahl (*The BFG, The Witches, Matilda,* and others)

Books by Kate DiCamillo (*Because of Winn-Dixie, The Tale of Despereaux, The Miraculous Journey of Edward Tulane*)

The Hundred Dresses by Eleanor Estes

The *Moffat* books by Eleanor Estes (*The Moffats, The Middle Moffat, Rufus M.*)

The Whipping Boy by Sid Fleischman

The Chronicles of Narnia by C. S. Lewis (*The Lion, the Witch and the Wardrobe* and other books in the series)

Sarah, Plain and Tall by Patricia MacLachlan
The Best Christmas Pageant Ever by Barbara Robinson
A Series of Unfortunate Events by Lemony Snicket is a fantastic series for building vocabulary.
The Boxcar Children by Gertrude Chandler Warner

GREAT EASY READER SERIES

These easy readers have multiple books with the same characters so your child can read lots of stories about each character.

Fly Guy by Ted Arnold is a series about a fly who becomes a pet (*Hi! Fly Guy, Super Fly Guy, Fly High, Fly Guy!*).
The *Biscuit* books by Alyssa Capucilli are an I Can Read series about a little yellow puppy (*Biscuit's Day at the Farm, Biscuit Goes to School, Biscuit and the Baby*).
Clark the Shark books by Bruce Hale have lots of rhymes and clear messages told in funny stories (*Clark the Shark: Too Many Treats, Clark the Shark: Lost and Found, Clark the Shark and the Big Book Report*).
The *Sofia Martinez* books (*Sofia Martinez: The Beach Trip*, and others) by Jacqueline Jules merge Spanish words with simple, relatable stories. These are great for readers who are building their stamina with reading.
Frog and Toad by Arnold Lobel is another classic series (*Frog and Toad Are Friends, Frog and Toad All Year, Frog and Toad Together, Days with Frog and Toad*).
Mouse Soup and *Mouse Tales* by Arnold Lobel have different stories collected in two books.
Little Bear by Else Holmelund Minarik (*A Kiss for Little Bear, Little Bear's Visit*).
The *Amelia Bedelia* books by Peggy Parish are I Can Read books with the grown-up Amelia Bedelia character (*Amelia Bedelia Goes Camping, Amelia Bedelia and the Baby, Calling Doctor Amelia Bedelia*) and the kid version (*Amelia Bedelia Goes Camping, Amelia Bedelia Is for the Birds, Amelia Bedelia Sleeps Over*).
Henry and Mudge books by Cynthia Rylant are a Ready to Read series (*Henry and Mudge in Puddle Trouble, Henry and Mudge in the Green Time, Henry and Mudge in the Sparkle Days*).
Nate the Great by Marjorie Weinman Sharmat is a good introduction to mystery stories (*Nate the Great and the Monster Mess, Nate the Great Goes Undercover, Nate the Great and the Stolen Base*).

CHAPTER BOOKS FOR YOUR CHILD TO READ ON THEIR OWN

These series are great ones for your child to check out. If they like one book, there are lots more to explore with each character.

Cam Jansen mysteries by David Adler (*Cam Jansen and the Mystery of the Stolen Diamonds, Cam Jansen: The Mystery of the Dinosaur Bones*)

The *Ivy and Bean* series by Annie Barrows are books about two friends (*Ivy and Bean and the Ghost That Had to Go, Ivy and Bean Break the Fossil Record*)

The *Fudge* books by Judy Blume (*Tales of a Fourth Grade Nothing, Superfudge*)*Flat Stanley* series by Jeff Brown (*Flat Stanley and the Magic Lamp, Flat Stanley's Worldwide Adventures: Lost in New York, Flat Stanley and the Very Big Cookie*)

The *Yasmin* books (*Meet Yasmin!, Yasmin the Superhero, Yasmin the Explorer*) by Saadia Faruqi

The Adventures of Pug (*Captain Pug, Safari Pug, Cowboy Pug*) by Laura James

Stink: The Incredible Shrinking Kid by Megan McDonald (*Stink and the World's Worst Super-Stinky Sneakers, Stink and the Incredible Super-Galactic Jawbreaker*)

Magic Tree House mysteries by Mary Pope Osborne (*Dinosaurs before Dark, The Knight at Dawn, Mummies in the Morning*)

Junie B. Jones series by Barbara Park (*Junie B. Jones and the Stupid Smelly Bus, Junie B. Jones, First Grader, Junie B., First Grader: Aloha-ha-ha,* and *Junie B., First Grader: Toothless Wonder*)

The *Clementine* series by Sara Pennypacker (*The Talented Clementine, Clementine and the Spring Trip*)

A to Z Mysteries by Ron Roy (*The Panda Puzzle, The Runaway Racehorse, Operation Orca*)

NONFICTION TO READ TOGETHER

There are lots of books about nonfiction topics that draw kids in and teach them basic and advanced information. These texts are a good place to start to learn about anything from animals to the human body.

Informational Texts to Read Together

The *Let's Read and Find Out* series (*What the Moon Is Like* by Franklyn Branley, *How a Seed Grows* by Helene Jordan)

The *You Wouldn't Want to . . .* series (You *Wouldn't Want to Live without Math* by Anne Rooney, *You Wouldn't Want to Be an American Colonist* by Jacqueline Morley)

Usborne Books (www.theusbornebookstore.com) publishes lots of different types of books for various ages on topics from the human body to space exploration.

The Magic School Bus books by Joanna Cole merge fiction and information and are a great starting point to learn about a topic. There are *Magic School Bus* books about dinosaurs, the water system, the human body, and lots of other topics.

Books by Dianna Aston are beautifully illustrated explorations of everything from seeds to butterflies (*A Beetle Is Shy, A Seed Is Sleepy, A Rock Is Lively, A Butterfly Is Patient,* and others).

Aliens from Earth: When Animals and Plants Invade Other Ecosystems by Mary Batten

Aaron and Alexander: The Most Famous Duel in American History by Don Brown

Gail Gibbons has written countless texts about the natural world, including *Tornadoes!*, *From Seed to Plant*, *Deserts*, *Alligators and Crocodiles*, *Ladybugs*, and more.

Water Land: Land and Water Forms around the World by Christy Hale

Worst of Friends: Thomas Jefferson, John Adams and the True Story of an American Feud by Suzanne Jurmain

This Is How We Do It: One Day in the Lives of Seven Kids from around the World by Matt Lamothe

Birthdays around the World by Margriet Ruurs

So You Want to Be President? by Judith St. George and David Small

A Place for Butterflies by Melissa Stewart

The Big Book of Beasts, *The Big Book of Bugs*, and *The Big Book of the Blue* by Yuval Zommer

Biographies to Read Together

Biographies are a great way to expand your child's knowledge about a topic with specific people and stories, or get your child interested in something new because of the powerful persona behind a topic. There are many powerful picture book biographies published today. Here is a selected list:

Counting on Katherine: How Katherine Johnson Saved Apollo 13 by Helaine Becker

Trombone Shorty by Troy Andrews

Manfish: A Story of Jacques Cousteau by Jennifer Berne

Nothing Stopped Sophie: The Story of Unshakeable Mathematician Sophie Germain by Cheryl Bordoe

Frida Kahlo and Her Animalitos by Monica Brown

Six Dots: A Story of Louis Braille by Jen Bryant

The Right Word: Roget and His Thesaurus by Jen Bryant

Planting Stories: The Life of Librarian and Storyteller Pura Belpré by Anika Denise

Tree Lady: The True Story of How One Tree-Loving Woman Changed a City Forever by H. Joseph Hopkins

Shark Lady: The True Story of How Eugenie Clark Became the Ocean's Most Fearless Scientist by Jess Keating

Snowflake Bentley by Jaqueline Briggs Martin

Brave Girl: Clara and the Shirtwaist Makers' Strike of 1909 by Michelle Merkel

The Girl Who Thought in Pictures: The Story of Dr. Temple Grandin by Julia Finley Mosca

Duke Ellington: The Piano Prince and His Orchestra by Andrea Pinkney

Dorothea's Eyes: Dorothea Lange Photographs the Truth by Barb Rosenstock

The Noisy Paint Box: The Colors and Sounds of Kandinsky's Abstract Art by Barb Rosenstock

Separate Is Never Equal: Sylvia Mendez and Her Family's Fight for Desegregation by Duncan Tonatiuh

Joan Procter, Dragon Doctor: The Woman Who Loved Reptiles by Patricia Valdez

Books about History to Read Together

Picture books are a great way to show your child important events in history, building background knowledge along the way. Here is a brief list of picture books about historical events and time periods.

The *Who Was* books are each about a famous figure in history (*Who Was Anne Frank?* by Ann Abramson, *Who Was Walt Disney?* by Whitney Stewart, and *Who Was Albert Einstein?* by Jess Brallier).

The *I Survived* books are about dramatic events in history (*I Survived the Battle of D-Day, 1944* and *I Survived the Attack of the Grizzlies, 1967*, both by Lauren Tarshis).

Children's Encyclopedia of American History by DK Publishing

Apples to Oregon by Deborah Hopkinson is a story of a family on the Oregon Trail.

The Cats in Krasinski Square by Karen Hesse is the story of a Jewish girl's involvement in the Resistance.

Sweet Clara and the Freedom Quilt by Deborah Hopkinson is a story about Clara, who lives on a plantation, and what happens when she learns about the Underground Railroad.

Hornbooks and Inkwells by Verla Kay is a story of life in an eighteenth-century one-room schoolhouse.

Dandelions by Eve Bunting tells the story of a family living in Nebraska Territory in the 1800s.

Baseball Saved Us by Ken Mochizuki is a picture book about life in a Japanese internment camp based on actual events.

Aunt Harriet's Underground Railroad in the Sky by Faith Ringgold tells the story of Harriet Tubman and the Underground Railroad.

Grandfather's Journey by Allen Say is a lyrical story about immigration.

Freedom Summer by Deborah Wiles is the story of Joe, who is White, and John Henry, who is Black, during the summer of 1964.

The Memory Coat by Elvira Woodruff tells the story of Ellis Island and the Russian immigrant experience.

This Is the Rope: A Story from the Great Migration by Jacqueline Woodson is the story of one girl who moved north during the Great Migration.

FUNNY BOOKS

Tom Angleberger's *Strange Case of Origami Yoda, Darth Paper Strikes Back, Princess Labelmaker to the Rescue!*

Jeff Kinney's *Diary of a Wimpy Kid* series (*The Third Wheel, Rodrick Rules, Double Down*)

Stan Kirby's *Captain Awesome* series (*Captain Awesome to the Rescue, Captain Awesome and the Easter Egg Bandit, Captain Awesome Takes a Dive*)

Lincoln Peirce's *Big Nate* series (*Big Nate: Hug It Out!, Big Nate: Payback Time!, Big Nate Goes Bananas!*)

Dav Pilkey's *Captain Underpants* and *Dog Man* series

Louis Sachar's *Holes* and *Sideways Stories from Wayside School* (series)

BOOKS THAT REFLECT DIVERSE EXPERIENCES

These lists focus on stories that reflect the history and experience of characters from various backgrounds and ethnicities.

African American

There are a lot of books that represent African American history and the experience very well. This list does not represent all of them, but a small collection of picture books and novels to start with.

Ron's Big Mission by Rose Blue is the story of Ron McNair, a nine-year-old who dreams of becoming an astronaut in 1959.

A Splash of Red: The Life and Art of Horace Pippin by Jen Bryant is the story of Horace Pippin, an artist who served in World War I.

Firebird by Misty Copeland connects Copeland's story to the aspirations of becoming a ballerina.

We March by Shane Evans tells the story of the 1963 march in Washington, DC, and Martin Luther King Jr.'s historic speech.

Midnight Teacher: Lilly Ann Granderson and Her Secret School by Janet Halfmann tells the story of Lilly Ann Granderson who learned to read and write as a slave and then shared her knowledge with other slaves despite the risks.

The People Could Fly: American Black Folktales by Virginia Hamilton, stories of folktales about hope, fantasy, animals, and the supernatural

Little Leaders: Bold Women in Black History by Vashti Harrison provides a snapshot of women who shaped Black history.

Wilma Unlimited: How Wilma Rudolph Became the World's Fastest Woman by Kathleen Krull, a biography of Wilma Rudolph who overcame polio to win the Olympics.

Henry's Freedom Box by Ellen Levine is a fictionalized account of Virginia slave Henry "Box" Brown and how he escaped to Philadelphia.

Jazz by Walter Dean Myers is the story of the beginnings of jazz music.

Harlem's Little Blackbird by Renee Watson is the story of Florence Mills, a Harlem Renaissance performer who inspired Black theater and musicals.

Hispanic

There are many books with Hispanic protagonists and about important people and events in Hispanic heritage. This is not an exhaustive list, but a place to start.

I Love Saturdays y domingos by Alma Flor Ada is the story of a girl who spends time with two sets of grandparents, one European American and one Mexican American.

The Secret Footprints by Julia Alvarez is a folktale of Ciguapas, a Dominican story about creatures who live underwater and only come out at night.

Portraits of Hispanic American Heroes by Juan Felipe Herrera tells the story of twenty notable Hispanic men and women.

Harvesting Hope: The Story of Cesar Chavez by Kathleen Krull is about Cesar Chavez, an activist who fought for the rights of American farmworkers.

Viva Frida by Yuyi Morales is the story of Frida Kahlo using a combination of photos and illustration.

Mango, Abuela, and Me by Meg Medina is about a little girl whose grandmother, Abuela, comes to stay with her. Abuela doesn't speak English so they find another way to form a bond.

The Princess and the Warrior: A Tale of Two Volcanos by Duncan Tonatiuh is an Aztec myth about two volcanos in Mexico and how they were formed.

Finding the Music by Jennifer Torres tells the story of a young Latina girl who breaks her grandfather's vihuela and discovers her grandfather's experience as a mariachi singer as she tries to fix it.

Sonia Sotomayor: A Judge Grows in the Bronx by Jonah Winter is the story of the first Hispanic Supreme Court justice.

Roberto Clemente: Pride of the Pittsburgh Pirates by Jonah Winter is a biography of a Hispanic baseball player who grew up in Puerto Rico and then became the first Latino baseball player in the Hall of Fame.

Asian

There are many books that share the Asian experience, and this is not an exhaustive list. For more information about books that reflect Asian experiences, check out the Colours of Us book list: https://coloursofus.com/30-asian-asian-american-childrens-books/.

Angkat: The Cambodian Cinderella by Jewell Coburn is the Cambodian take on the fairy tale.

Henry and the Kite Dragon by Bruce Hall is a story of how children from two different groups come together.

Sadako and the Thousand Paper Cranes by Eleanor Coerr is the story of a girl who survived the bombing of Hiroshima and developed leukemia later in life. She makes paper cranes in hopes that she will get better.

The *Ling and Ting* books by Grace Ling tell the story of two twins who look the same but are very different (*Ling and Ting: Not Exactly the Same!*, *Ling and Ting Share a Birthday*, *Ling and Ting: Twice as Silly*).

The Seven Chinese Brothers by Margaret Mahy is a Chinese folktale about seven brothers who use their gifts to overpower an evil emperor.

The *Katie Woo* books by Fran Manushkin are stories about an adventurous girl (*No More Teasing*, *Boss of the World*, *Too Much Rain*).

Red Butterfly: How a Princess Smuggled the Secret of Silk out of China by Deborah Noyes is the story of a brave Chinese princess who has to marry a prince and leave her home behind.

Sparrow Girl by Sara Pennypacker is the story of Ming-Li and her village's efforts to keep the sparrows in China after they ate too much grain and were banished.

Suki's Kimono by Chieri Uegaki is the story of Suki, who loves her kimono and gets to share her kimono and her experience of visiting her grandmother with her classmates on her first day back at school.

Native American

This is a starting list of Native American books that you can read with your child.

Chester Nez and the Unbreakable Code: A Navajo Code Talker's Story by Joseph Bruchac is the story of Chester Nez, who was called on to use the Navajo language to create a code during World War II.

The People Shall Continue by Simon Ortiz is the story of how indigenous people have endured in the face of European colonization.

When We Were Alone by David Robertson is the story of a young girl who discovers why her grandmother dresses and speaks in ways that celebrates her Cree heritage.

We Are Grateful: Otsaliheliga by Traci Sorell is an introduction to the expression of small joys and gratitude in the Cherokee nation.

Tallchief: America's Prima Ballerina by Maria Tallchief is the story of Maria Tallchief who was raised on an Osage Indian reservation and grew up to become a prima ballerina.

Arabic

One Green Apple by Eve Bunting is the story of a new immigrant who finds that there are some things that are familiar in her new country.

Lailah's Lunchbox: A Ramadan Story by Reem Faruqi is the story of how one girl celebrates Ramadan and makes friends who appreciate her beliefs.

Saffron Ice Cream by Rashin Kheiriyeh tells the story of Rashin who is excited about visiting the beach in her new home and remembers her former trips to the beach in Iran.

Under the Ramadan Moon by Sylvia Whitman introduces children to the monthlong observance of Ramadan.

Four Feet, Two Sandals by Karen Williams introduces children to the refugee experience.

Malala's Magic Pencil by Malala Yousafzai is a book that introduces children to the story of Malala Yousafzai, an advocate for girl's education.

Indian

Finders Keepers? A Bus Trip in India by Robert Arnett and Smita Turakhia explores what Arnett learned during his travels in India.

Aru Shah and the End of Time by Roshani Chokshi is a story inspired by Hindu mythology, about a twelve-year-old girl who starts a cosmic showdown when she lights a lamp.

Grandma and the Great Gourd by Chitra Banerjee Divakaruni is a Bengali folktale about a grandma and her loyal dogs, Kalu and Bhulu, and how they outwit jungle animals.

Elephant Dance: A Journey to India by Theresa Heine and Sheila Moxley tells the story of how Ravi and Anjali's grandfather remembers India.

Chachaji's Cup by Uma Krishnaswami and Soumya Sitaraman is the story of how a boy and his uncle spend their time, particularly teatime, through the story of a treasured teacup.

POETRY COLLECTIONS

Poetry is a great way to read something funny or lyrical. Start with these poetry collections.

Where the Sidewalk Ends and other books by Shel Silverstein

Jack Prelutsky has written poetry collections for kids, including *The New Kid on the Block* and *Something Big Has Been Here.*

The Random House Book of Poetry for Children by Jack Prelutsky

The *Poetry for Kids* series has collections of poems curated for kids by Robert Frost, Emily Dickinson, Maya Angelou, and other poets.

Honey, I Love by Eloise Greenfield

All the Colors of the Earth by Sheila Hamanaka

Keep a Pocket in Your Poem by J. Patrick Lewis

Feel the Beat: Dance Poems that Zing from Salsa to Swing by Marilyn Singer

A Child's Anthology of Poetry by Elizabeth Sword

Brown Honey in Broomwheat Tea by Joyce Carol Thomas

Thunder Underground by Jane Yolen

Appendix B
Frequently Asked Questions

Active Reading is something that, as you read to your child who is growing and changing, will grow and change, too. You may have lots of questions that weren't answered within the chapters of this book. That's where this section comes in. These are questions that extend beyond the basics of the ABCs.

How do you find the time to read aloud to your children?

Like many things in parenting, you stop what you're doing and focus on your child when they need something; in this case, they need books. You can also think about how to work Active Reading into your day. Try planning backward to include reading into every bedtime. If your kids need to be in bed by 7:30 p.m., plan from there to figure out what time they need to brush teeth, eat dinner, and read books and still get into bed on time. You can also read to your kids during bath time and other little moments you can steal during the evening.

If you want more time in your schedule for reading, find time by limiting after-school and weekend activities and thinking about other areas of the day or week that you can "steal" time for reading later. For example, can you assign a daily task to your children to free up time from housework? That's not to say that it's easy to find time to read every day, but thinking about time as a commodity and how to save it may help you find more time to read.

Should I read aloud to my child who has a disability? What about longer books and chapter books?

There are many different types of disability, but the primary types of disability that may affect how a child engages with literature include cognitive delay, speech impairment, and hearing loss, as well as language disabilities.

For all these, the short answer to this is yes! Do not shy away from reading complex books to children, regardless of whether or not they have a disability. Reading picture books and even chapter books to children with disabilities exposes them to rich language, new words, and interesting ideas. As you read with your child, as you would with any child, look and listen to see how they are engaging with the book. They may not grasp onto the same aspects that you notice, but that's okay.

How can I help my child who has a reading or language disability build language, vocabulary, and comprehension skills through Active Reading?

Talking about story grammar helps children develop an understanding of how stories work. For students who have a disability that affects their reading comprehension or language, having conversations about story structure, and even mapping out what happens during a story using pictures, can help them develop an understanding of story grammar that supports later comprehension. Reading with a child with a disability, you may ask more story questions and provide more help visualizing what is happening. You may also read more picture books and chapter books than novels. That's okay! The point is to enjoy stories and books together, not to reach a certain level of book.

I have children of different ages. Can I read to them at the same time?

This is a common concern and a question that I get asked a lot. As a parent with three kids of differing ages myself, I know the struggle. There are two approaches that you can use: divide and conquer, or trend toward the middle.

Divide and conquer. If you have multiple children and multiple caregivers at home, when possible, split the bedtime reading duties up and have each parent read to one child. It might not happen every night because of work schedules and other commitments, but when you can, each child gets to choose what they want to read and have one-on-one time with one of their caregivers.

When you can't divide and conquer your kids among adults, you can also divide and conquer the book selection. Having each child choose a book and reading one chapter or section from each of them is another way to divide the reading among your children. Rest assured that reading a book that is "too high" or "too low" is not a big deal. Chances are, your younger child can get something from listening to a higher book, and your older child can enjoy listening to a familiar story.

Trend toward the middle. In my house, bedtime reading can be a one-parent job. So I focus on choosing a read-aloud that we can all enjoy—a chapter book that may be right at my younger daughter's level even if my older daughter could listen to something higher. Then we choose a picture book or two, which is where we do most of the Active Reading because we can talk about the text (for my older daughter) and the pictures (for my younger daughter). Finally, we choose one easy reader for my oldest to read to us, giving her time to practice reading and giving her sister an opportunity to enjoy another story.

How do I choose books for family read-alouds when I have kids who are different ages?

First, recall that children's listening comprehension skills are higher than their reading ability until middle school. So you can choose books that all your kids can enjoy, even if it feels "too high" for your younger child. Illustrated chapter books, like *Dory Fantasmagory* by Abby Hanlon and *Mercy Watson* by Kate DiCamillo, are good choices for pairs of kids who are old enough to follow a longer picture book, but one child needs more pictures to understand the story. And sticking with picture books that have complex themes but are still comprehensible by younger children is also a good way to keep reading together. *Last Stop on Market Street* by Matt de la Peña, *Islandborn* by Junot Diaz, and many classic fairy tales are good examples. It's also okay to have each child choose a book they want to read and engage the other in the ABCs, even if the book may seem too high or too low.

How can I do Active Reading with a child who doesn't like to read?

First, Active Reading techniques do not have to be done just with books (see Chapter 10). Think about ways that you can engage your child in the important thinking that comes with the ABCs of Active Reading outside of books. Then try to segue your child into books using their interests or the social aspects of reading. What books are their friends reading? What books do they hear about on the playground that they'd like to read?

You may also return to "comfort books." Comfort books are those that are not vocabulary rich and may not even really be a story (think *Where's Waldo?* or even lift-the-flap books), but that have sentimental value for your kids. There's no problem reading books that are at a lower level than your kids' abilities; in fact, it's a good thing if it keeps your kids reading and interested in books, and maintains the fun aspect of reading.

I speak a language at home that's different than the one my child is learning at school. Should I read to my child in our home language?

Short answer: Yes! Reading to a child in the language they're learning at home (or in school) builds important language skills that support their comprehension. In fact, reading and talking in your home language supports your child's language skills as effectively as reading and talking in the language they use at school.[1]

In fact, reading in your child's home language will help them make connections between their school and home language. Hearing words in books or in conversation in both languages helps children learn. Research on dialogic reading with children who were learning two languages indicated that children who were learning English and who engaged in dialogic reading had stronger vocabulary.[2]

Is listening to an audiobook the same as Active Reading?

Audiobooks are a great option when you're in the car or can't sit down together. They are also a great way for children who struggle with reading, such as children who have dyslexia, to engage with complex text on their own. But unless you're stopping the audiobook every so often to talk about the story, and have the book in front of you while the recording reads the words, you're not going to get the same benefits as Active Reading. That said, when you listen to audiobooks, stopping after every chapter or section to talk about what happened and make predictions about what may happen next can add to your child's comprehension.

What do I do if I come across a topic or idea I don't agree with in a book?

First, it's okay to preview what you read with your child before you sit down together. If a topic does not align with your family values, it's okay to shelve it for a while. If the book is something that your child is very interested in, it may be worth it to start talking about the topic and your family's views on it. Start with story questions, to gauge what your child understands from the book and from their background knowledge. Then use the story as a starting point to talk about what experiences you've had with this topic, and what your family's perspective is. And always leave room for your child to ask their own questions.

How do I introduce my child to more controversial topics using Active Reading?

There are many times that books and stories may be the best way to start a conversation about a topic that's in the news, or that you have an opinion about and want to develop your child's knowledge around. These topics often seem too abstract to just explain—how do we explain war or death to a six-year-old?

To introduce your child to a controversial or sensitive topic, find books that introduce the topic clearly and simply. For example, to introduce the topic of refugees and immigration, you may read *The Journey* by Francesca Sanna and *Dreamers* by Yuyi Morales. Both of these stories include information about why people leave their home countries, but they also offer hope and resolution, which is helpful for kids. As you read about new topics, ask simple questions to make sure your child understands the basics and empha-size empathy building with questions like, How do you think they felt? Have you ever felt that way? And use text features or other information to build background knowledge. For example, look at maps to show how countries are connected to understand how people move from one country to another. If your child seems uninterested in or overwhelmed by the topic you're talking about, it's okay to pull back and stop reading about it. When they're ready and interested, you can return to the books and conversation.

My child wants to read a story that I find absolutely boring, or they are interested in a topic that I just cannot get into. How do I connect with what we're reading?

Unfortunately, this is a common problem. I've read many books that are tedious and boring to me (and that my children ask to read again and again). Lessen the tedium for you by:

- Asking your child: What do you like about this book? What is interest-ing to you about this? Find out what they like about it and try to see it through their eyes.
- Finding an intersection between your interests and theirs. Particularly with nonfiction, can you find a way to experience the topic they love us-ing something that interests you? If they are in love with horses and you enjoy art, can you find a way to merge those two interests?
- Help your child find books they can read on their own. As your child learns to read on their own, exploring their own interests and favorites, from favorite characters to hobbies, is a great way for them to experience the joys of being an independent reader. After they read, ask them to tell you about the story or topic.

Once my child is reading well on their own, how do I balance encourag-ing them to read and reading to them?

It is a balance. Once children have mastered the reading basics, they're still building stamina and may not want to read for very long. So having them choose one "you read to me" book may be enough for bedtime reading; the rest can be "I read to you." I try to have my daughter read at least one book to me every day to make it a habit, but I often make it a suggestion, not "homework" or a demand. Also, doing a mix of picture books that allow your child to relax and enjoy the pictures and chapter books that build their listen-ing stamina (as well as encourage them to listen to lots of different, longer stories) will spill over into their reading on their own. So even when they're not reading to you they're still benefiting.

What if my child, who can read on their own, doesn't want me to read to them? They want to read on their own.

That's okay! They're probably excited about their new reading skills and feel like they can do it! If you want to continue reading aloud with them, I suggest taking them to the library and looking at novels that are intriguing to them based on the cover or genre. Also, books that you enjoyed as a child may be good because you can share your memories of those books.

What if my child doesn't want me to do Active Reading? What if they don't want me to ask questions or talk about what we read?

This is another common occurrence. When this happens—your child stops you from asking questions and tells you to "just read"—take the opportunity to just read! You can always talk about the story afterward, or pick up Active Reading when they are interested in it. There's nothing wrong with just enjoying a book read aloud.

How do I know a book is too hard? Or how do I know that I shouldn't read this book to my child?

Of course, it's important to gauge your child's ability to deal with new vocabulary. *Matilda* may be over your child's head for the moment because of the many challenging vocabulary words; that's okay. In this case, read a book with more modern language, like *Dory Fantasmagory*, or one that has a simpler storyline, like *Stuart Little*. You can always return to *Matilda* later.

What do I do if my child wants to read a book that I think is too scary for them?

Many topics that we read about can be scary. But our perception of what is scary may not be the same as our child. Let your child take the lead. Preview the book and if the cover or pictures are too scary, put it down. If you're reading and your child says that it's too scary, put it down. But if your child is interested and comfortable, they may be able to tolerate more thrill than you thought.

How will I know if my child is benefiting in school from the Active Reading we're doing at home?

Active Reading will influence your child's vocabulary, comprehension, and love of books. Some questions that you can ask your child's teacher that will give you insight into how the Active Reading is influencing reading at school include:

- Tell me about how my child does during class read-aloud.

- Tell me about how my child does during class discussion.
- Is my child able to understand what they read? How do you know?
- What does my child do when they're interested in a topic? What do you notice?
- What does my child do when they start a new book?

How do I make sure my child is understanding what they read when they are reading entirely on their own?

When your child is reading an easy reader, chapter book, or novel on their own, ask them story questions to learn what the book is about and ensure they are understanding it. When your child can answer questions about what happened and why, they're following the story of the book! Three questions that you can always ask about fiction are:

- What happened in the story?
- What was your favorite part?
- Who else might like that book and why?

Questions that you can always ask about nonfiction include:

- What did you learn?
- What was the most interesting thing that you learned?
- What questions do you have about that topic now?

Where can I go for more information about Active Reading?

Active Reading was originally created through work with Read Charlotte, a nonprofit organization in Charlotte, North Carolina. You can find out more about Active Reading through their web site and efforts: www.readcharlotte .org

The Campaign for Grade Level Reading has information about helping children master reading by third grade and efforts around the country: www .gradelevelreading.net

Brightly has book lists and recommendations: www.readbrightly.com

Reading Rockets is a site by WETA Public Television with lots of information about reading: www.readingrockets.org. It also has a bilingual site in Spanish with information about reading with kids: www.colorincolorado.org

Notes

INTRODUCTION

1. Hernandez, D. J. (2011). *Double jeopardy: How third grade reading skills and poverty influence high school graduation.* Baltimore, MD: Annie E. Casey Foundation.

2. Lonigan, C. J., & Whitehurst, G. J. (1998). Relative efficacy of parent and teacher involvement in a shared-reading intervention for preschool children from low-income backgrounds. *Early Childhood Research Quarterly, 13*(2), 263–290; Wasik, B. A., & Bond, M. A. (2001). Beyond the pages of a book: Interactive book reading and language development in pre-school classrooms. *Journal of Educational Psychology, 93*(2), 243–250; Whitehurst, G. J., Arnold, D. S., Epstein, J. N., Angell, A. L., Smith, M., & Fischel, J. E. (1994). A picture book reading intervention in day care and home for children from low-income families. *Developmental Psychology, 30*(5), 679–689.

3. Trelease, J. (2013). *The read-aloud handbook* (7th ed.). New York, NY: Penguin Books.

4. Mackenzie, S. (2018). *The read-aloud family: Making meaningful and lasting connections with your kids.* Grand Rapids, MI: Zondervan.

5. Scholastic. (2016). *Kids and family reading report.* Retrieved from https://www.scholastic.com/readingreport/home.html

6. Trelease, 2013.

7. Konrath, S. H., O'Brien, E. H., & Hsing, C. (2010). Changes in dispositional empathy in American college students over time: A meta-analysis. *Personality and Social Psychology Review, 15*(2), 180–198.

8. Trelease, 2013.

CHAPTER 1

1. Cleaver, S., & Richardson, M. (2018). *Read with me: Engaging your young child in Active Reading.* Lanham, MD: Rowman & Littlefield.

2. Hutton, J., Xu, Y., DeWitt, T., Horowitz-Kraus, T., & Ittenbach, R. (2018). Goldilocks effect? Illustrated story format seems "just right" and animation "too hot" for integration of functional brain networks in preschool-aged children. Pediatric Academic Societies, Toronto, Canada. https://www.eurekalert.org/pub_releases /2018-05/pas-nsm042618.php

3. The research on preschool read aloud is detailed in Cleaver & Richardson, 2018.

4. National Reading Panel. (2000). *Report of the National Reading Panel. Teaching children to read: An evidence-based assessment of the scientific research literature on reading and its implications for reading instruction* (NIH Publication No. 00-4769). Washington, DC: US Government Printing Office.

5. Adams, M. J. (1990). *Beginning to read: Thinking and learning about print.* Cambridge, MA: MIT Press; Hoover, W. A., & Gough, P. B. (1999). The simple view of reading. *Reading and Writing: An Interdisciplinary Journal, 2,* 127–160.

6. Storch, S. A., & Whitehurst, G. J. (2002). Oral language and code-related precursors to reading: Evidence from a longitudinal structural model. *Developmental Psychology, 38,* 934–947.

7. Hutton et al., 2018.

8. Torgesen, J., & Davis, C. (1996). Individual difference variables that predict response to training in phonological awareness. *Journal of Experimental Child Psychology, 63,* 1–21; Storch & Whitehurst, 2002.

9. Storch & Whitehurst, 2002.

10. Roth, F. P., Speece, D. L., & Cooper, D. H. (2002). A longitudinal analysis of the connection between oral language and early reading. *The Journal of Education Research, 95*(5), 259–272.

11. Roth et al., 2002.

12. Nation, K., & Snowling, M. J. (1998). Semantic processing and the development of word-recognition skills: Evidence from children with reading comprehension difficulties. *Journal of Memory and Language, 39,* 85–101.

13. Hogan, T. P., Adlof, S. M., & Alonzo, C. (2014). On the importance of listening comprehension. *Journal of Speech Language Pathology, 16*(3), 199–207.

14. Hogan et al., 2014.

15. Dickinson, D. K., & Smith, M. W. (1994). Long-term effects of preschool teachers' book readings on low-income children's vocabulary and story comprehension. *Reading Research Quarterly, 29,* 104–122.

16. Smolkin, L. B., & Donovan, C. A. (2001). The contexts of comprehension: The information book read-aloud, comprehension acquisition, and comprehension instruction in a first-grade classroom. *Elementary School Journal, 102,* 97–122.

17. Cain, K., & Oakhill, J. (2006b). Profiles of children with specific reading comprehension difficulties. *British Journal of Educational Psychology, 76*(4), 683–696.

18. Oakhill, J. V., & Cain, K. (2012). The precursors of reading ability in young readers: Evidence from a four-year longitudinal study. *Scientific Studies of Reading, 16*(2), 91–121.

CHAPTER 2

1. Wolf, M. (2018). *Reader, Come Home.* New York, NY: HarperCollins.

2. Wolf, 2018.

3. Also known as the simple view of reading; Hoover, W. A., & Gough, P. B. (1999). The simple view of reading. *Reading and Writing: An Interdisciplinary Journal, 2,* 127–160.

4. de Jong, P. F., & van der Leij, A. (2002). Effects of phonological abilities and linguistic comprehension on the development of reading. *Scientific Studies of Reading, 6,* 51–77.

5. Cain, K., Catts, H., Hogan, T., & Loma, R., Language and Reading Research Consortium. (2015). Learning to read: Should we keep things simple? *Reading Research Quarterly, 50,* 151–169; Tilstra, J., McMaster, K., van den Broek, P., Kendeou, P., & Rapp, D. (2009). Simple but complex: Components of the simple view of reading across grade levels. *Journal of Research in Reading, 32,* 383–401.

6. Catts, H. W. (2018). The simple view of reading: Advancements and false impressions. *Remedial and Special Education, 39,* 317–323.

7. Pearson, D. P., Valencia, S. W., & Wixson, K. (2014). Complicating the world of reading assessment: Toward better assessments for better teaching. *Theory into Practice, 53,* 236–246.

8. Tamer, M. T., & Walsh, B. 2016. *Raising strong readers: Strategies for parents and educators to encourage children to read from infancy to high school.* Retrieved from www.gse.harvard.edu/news/uk/16/03/raising-strong-readers

9. Tamer & Walsh, 2016.

10. Liu, Y., Liu, H., & Hau, K. (2016). Reading ability development from kindergarten to junior secondary: Latent transition analyses with growth mixture modeling. *Frontier Psychology, 7.*

11. Verhoeven, L., van Leeuwe, J., & Vermeer, A. (2011). Vocabulary growth and reading development across the elementary school years. *Scientific Studies of Reading, 15,* 8–25.

12. Verhoeven et al., 2011.

13. Catts, H. W., Hogan, T., & Adlof, S. (2005). Developmental changes in reading and reading disabilities. In H. Catts & A. Kamhi (Eds.), *Connections between language and reading disabilities* (pp. 25–40). Mahwah, NJ: Lawrence Erlbaum, Language and Reading Research Consortium.

14. National Reading Panel. (2000). *Report of the National Reading Panel. Teaching children to read: An evidence-based assessment of the scientific research literature on reading and its implications for reading instruction* (NIH Publication No. 00-4769). Washington, DC: US Government Printing Office.

15. Tankersly, K. (2003). *The threads of reading.* Alexandria, VA: Association for Supervision and Curriculum Development.

16. Adams, M. J. (1990). *Beginning to read: Thinking and learning about print.* Cambridge, MA: MIT Press; Anderson, R. C., Hiebert, E. H., Scott, J. A., & Wilkinson, I. A. S. (1985). *Becoming a nation of readers: The report of the Commission on Reading.* National Institute of Education. Washington, DC: Department of Education; Snow, C. E., Burns, S., & Griffin, P. (Eds.). (1998). *Preventing reading difficulties in young children.* Washington, DC: National Academies Press.

17. Cleaver, S. & Richardson, M. (2018). *Read with me: Engaging your young reader in Active Reading.* Lanham, MD: Rowman & Littlefield.

18. National Reading Panel, 2000.

19. Wolf, 2018.

20. Roth, F. P., Speece, D. L., & Cooper, D. H. (2002). A longitudinal analysis of the connection between oral language and early reading. *The Journal of Education Research, 95*(5), 259–272.

21. Roth et al., 2002.

22. Connor, C. M., Spencer, M., Day, S. L., Giuliani, S., Ingebrand, S. W., Mclean, L., & Morrison, F. J. (2014). Capturing the complexity: Content, type, and amount of instruction and quality of the classroom learning environment synergistically predict third graders' vocabulary and reading comprehension outcomes. *Journal of Educational Psychology, 106,* 762–778.

23. Dickinson, D. K., & Smith, M. W. (1994). Long-term effects of preschool teachers' book readings on low-income children's vocabulary and story comprehension. *Reading Research Quarterly, 29,* 104–122; Lever, R., & Senechal, M. (2011). Discussing stories: On how dialogic reading intervention improves kindergarteners' narrative construction. *Journal of Experimental Child Psychology, 108,* 1–24; Smolkin, L. B., & Donovan, C. A. (2001).The contexts of comprehension: The information book read-aloud, comprehension acquisition, and comprehension instruction in a first-grade classroom. *Elementary School Journal, 102,* 97–122.

24. Smolkin & Donovan, 2001.

25. Smolkin & Donovan, 2001; Brabham, E. G., & Lynch-Brown, C. (2002). Effects of teachers' reading-aloud styles on vocabulary acquisition and comprehension of students in the early elementary grades. *Journal of Educational Psychology, 94,* 465–473.

26. Wolf, 2018.

27. Hoover & Gough, 1999.

28. Bowey, J. A. (1986). Syntactic awareness in relation to reading skills and on-going reading comprehension monitoring. *Journal of Experimental Child Psychology, 41,* 282–299; Klecan-Aker, J. S., & Caraway, T. H. (1997). A study of the relationship of storytelling ability and reading comprehension in fourth and sixth grade: African American children. *European Journal of Disorders of Communication, 32,* 109–125.

29. Storch, S. A., & Whitehurst, G. J. (2002). Oral language and code-related precursors to reading: Evidence from a longitudinal structural model. *Developmental Psychology, 38,* 934–947.

30. Catts, H. W., Fey, M. E., Zhang, X., & Tomblin, J. B. (1999). Language basis of reading and reading disabilities: Evidence from a longitudinal investigation. *Scientific Studies of Reading, 3,* 331–361; Nation, K., & Snowling, M. J. (1998). Semantic processing and the development of word-recognition skills: Evidence from children with reading comprehension difficulties. *Journal of Memory and Language, 39,* 85–101.

31. Nation & Snowling, 1998.

32. Mol, S. E., Bus, A. G., & de Jong, M. T. (2009). Interactive book reading in early education: A tool to stimulate print knowledge as well as oral language. *Review of Educational Research, 79,* 979–1007; Swanson, E., Wanzek, J., Petscher, Y., Vaughn, S., Heckert, J., Cavanaugh, C., Kraft, G., & Tackett, K. (2011). A synthesis of read-aloud interventions on early reading outcomes among preschool through third graders at risk for reading difficulties. *Journal of Learning Disabilities, 44,* 258–275.

33. Wise, J. C., Sevcik, R. A., Morris, R. D., Lovett, M. W., & Wolf, M. (2007). The relationship among receptive and expressive vocabulary, listening comprehension, pre-reading skills, word identification skills, and reading comprehension by children with reading disabilities. *Journal of Speech, Language, and Hearing Research, 50,* 1093–1109.

34. Wise et al., 2007.

35. Nye, C., Turner, H., & Schwartz, J. (2006). *Approaches to parent involvement for improving the academic performance of elementary school age children.* Oslo, Norway: Campbell Collaboration.

36. Warren, C., Edwards, D., Isenberg, S., & Oldani, J. (2010). Effects of at-home reading activities and parental involvement on classroom reading scores: Focus on the Elementary Years. Available from ProQuest Dissertations.

37. Snow et al., 1998.

38. Egalite, A. J. (2016). How family background influences student achievement. *Education Next, 16*(2). Retrieved from https://www.educationnext.org/how-family-background-influences-student-achievement/

39. de Jong, P. F., & Leseman, P. P. M. (2001). Lasting effects of home literacy on reading achievement at school. *Journal of School Psychology, 39*(5), 389–414.

CHAPTER 3

1. Evans, M. D. R., Kelley, J., & Sikora, J. (2014). Scholarly culture and academic performance in 42 nations. *Social Forces, 92,* 1573–1605.

2. Hutton, J., Xu, Y., DeWitt, T., Horowitz-Kraus, T., & Ittenbach, R. (2018, May). Goldilocks effect? Illustrated story format seems "just right" and animation "too hot" for integration of functional brain networks in preschool-aged children. Pediatric Academic Societies, Toronto, Canada. https://www.eurekalert.org/pub_releases/2018-05/pas-nsm042618.php

3. Trelease, J. (2013). *The read-aloud handbook* (7th ed.). New York, NY: Penguin.

4. Fleming, J., Capatano, S., Thompson, C. M., & Carrillo, S. R. (2016). *More mirrors in the classroom: Using urban children's literature to increase literacy.* Lanham, MD: Rowman & Littlefield.

5. Huyck, D., & Dahlen, S. P. (2019). Diversity in children's books 2018. *Sarah park.com* blog. Created in consultation with Edith Campbell, Molly Beth Griffin, K. T. Horning, Debbie Reese, Ebony Elizabeth Thomas, and Madeline Tyner, with statistics compiled by the Cooperative Children's Book Center, School of Education, University of Wisconsin-Madison: ccbc.education.wisc.edu/books/pcstats.asp. Retrieved from https://readingspark.wordpress.com/2019/06/19/picture-this-diversity -in-childrens-books-2018-infographic/

6. Epstein, B. J. (2017, February 6). Why children's books that teach diversity are more important than ever. *The Conversation.* Retrieved from https://theconversation .com/why-childrens-books-that-teach-diversity-are-more-important-than-ever-72146

7. Epstein, 2017.

8. Epstein, 2017.

9. Wolf, M. (2018). *Reader, come home.* New Yor, NY: HarperCollins.

CHAPTER 4

1. Anderson, R. C., Nguyen-Jahiel, K., McNurlen, B., Archodidou, A., Kim, S., Reznitskaya, A., et al. (2001). The snowball phenomenon: Spread of ways of talking and ways of thinking across groups of children. *Cognition and Instruction, 19,* 1–46.

2. Wegerif, R., Mercer, N., & Dawes, L. (1999). From social interaction to individual reasoning: An empirical investigation of a possible sociocultural model of cognitive development. *Learning and Instruction, 9,* 493–516.

3. Reznitskaya, A., Anderson, R. C., McNurlen, B., Nguyen-Jahiel, K., Archodidou, A., & Kim, S. (2001). Influence of oral discussion on written argument. *Discourse Processes, 32,* 155–175.

4. Nir, S. M. (2018, November 5). Mystery in a small town: Couple shot dead, their daughter missing. *New York Times.* Retrieved from https://www.nytimes .com/2018/11/05/us/jayme-closs-missing-girl-barron-wisconsin.html?action =click&module=Top%20Stories&pgtype=Homepage

5. Jackson, S. (1948/2009). The lottery. In *The lottery and other stories.* New York, NY: Penguin. (Original work published in *The New Yorker* magazine on June 26, 1948.)

6. Baker, L., & Stein, N. (1981). The development of prose comprehension skills. In C. Santa & B. Hayes (Eds.), *Children's prose comprehension: Research and practice* (pp. 7–43). Newark, DE: International Reading Association; Nelson-Herber, J., & Johnston, C. S. (1989). Questions and concerns about teaching narrative and expository text. In K. D. Muth (Ed.), *Children's comprehension of text: Research into practice* (pp. 263–280). Newark, DE: International Reading Association.

7. Anderson, R. C. (1984). Role of reader's schema in comprehension, learning, and memory. In R. C. Anderson, J. Osborn, & R. Tierney (Eds.), *Learning to read in American schools: Basal readers and content texts* (pp. 243–257). Hillsdale, NJ: Lawrence Erlbaum.

8. Anderson, J. R., Finchem, J. L., & Douglass, S. (1997). The role of examples and rules in the acquisition of a cognitive skill. *Journal of Experimental Psychology: Learning, Memory and Cognition, 23,* 932–945; Bransford, J. D., & Johnson, M. K. (1972). Contextual prerequisites for understanding: Some investigations of comprehension and recall. *Journal of Verbal Learning and Verbal Behavior, 11,* 717–726.

9. Dymock, S. (2007). Comprehension strategy instruction: Teaching narrative text structure awareness. *The Reading Teacher, 61*(2).

10. Trabasso, T. (1981). Can we integrate research and instruction on reading comprehension? In C. Santa & B. Hayes (Eds.), *Children's prose comprehension: Research and practice* (pp. 103–116). Newark, DE: International Reading Association.

11. Trabasso, T., & Wiley, J. (2005). Goal plans of action and inferences during comprehension of narratives. *Discourse Processes, 39,* 129–164.

12. van den Broek, P., Kendeou, P., Kremer, K., Lynch, J., Butler, J., White, M. J., et al. (2005). Assessment of comprehension abilities in young children. In S. G. Paris & S. A. Stahl (Eds.), *Children's reading comprehension and assessment* (pp. 107–130). Mahwah, NJ: Lawrence Erlbaum.

13. Baumann, J. F., & Bergeron, B. S. (1993). Story map instruction using children's literature: Effects on first graders' comprehension of central narrative elements. *Journal of Reading Behavior, 25,* 407–437.

14. Calfee, R. C., & Patrick, C. L. (1995). *Teach our children well: Bringing K–12 education into the 21st century.* Stanford, CA: Stanford Alumni.

15. Lever, R., & Senechal, M. (2011). Discussing stories: On how dialogic reading intervention improves kindergarteners' narrative construction. *Journal of Experimental Child Psychology, 108,* 1–24.

16. Dymock, 2007.

17. Fisher, D., & Frey, N. (2016, February 15). Questioning that deepens comprehension. *Edutopia.* Retrieved from https://www.edutopia.org/blog/questioning-that -deepens-comprehension-douglas-fisher-nancy-frey.

18. Fisher & Frey, 2016.

19. Dickinson, D. K., & Smith, M. W. (1994). Long-term effects of preschool teachers' book readings on low-income children's vocabulary and story comprehension. *Reading Research Quarterly, 29,* 104–122.

20. Brabham, E. G., & Lynch-Brown, C. (2002). Effects of teachers' reading-aloud styles on vocabulary acquisition and comprehension of students in the early elementary grades. *Journal of Educational Psychology, 94,* 465–473.

21. Zwiers, J., & Crawford, M. (2011). *Academic conversations: Classroom talk that fosters critical thinking and content understanding.* Portsmouth, NH: Stenhouse.

CHAPTER 5

1. Cunningham, A. E., & Stanovich, K. E. (1997). Early reading acquisition and its relation to reading experience and ability 10 years later. *Developmental Psychology, 33,* 934–945.

2. Nagy, W. & Anderson, R. C. (1984). How many words are there in printed school English? *Reading Research Quarterly, 19,* 304–330.

3. Baker, S., Simmons, D., & Kame'enui, E. (1998). *Vocabulary acquisition: Synthesis of the research.* Washington, DC: U.S. Department of Education, Office of Educational Research and Improvement, Educational Resources Information Center; Beck, I. L., Perfetti, C. A., & McKeown, M. G. (1982). The effects of long-term vocabulary instruction on lexical access and reading comprehension. *Journal of Educational Psychology, 74,* 506–521.

4. Cain, K., Oakhill, J., & Lemmon, K. (2004). Individual differences in the inference of word meanings from context: The influence of reading comprehension, vocabulary knowledge, and memory capacity. *Journal of Educational Psychology, 964,* 671–681.

5. Cain, K., & Oakhill, J. (2006a). Matthew effects in young readers: Reading comprehension and reading experience aid vocabulary development. *Journal of Learning Disabilities, 44,* 431–443.

6. Beck, I. L., McKeown, M. G., & Kucan, L. (2013). *Bringing words to life* (2nd ed.). New York, NY: Guilford.

7. Nagy, W., Herman, P., & Anderson, R. C. (1985). Learning words from context. *Reading Research Quarterly, 20,* 233–253; Swaburn, M. S. L., & de Glopper, K. (1999). Incidental word learning while reading: A meta-analysis. *Review of Educational Research, 69,* 261–285.

8. Beck et al., 2013.

9. Duff, D., Tomblin, J. B., & Catts, H. (2015). The influence of reading on vocabulary growth: A case for a Matthew effect. *Journal of Speech, Language, and Hearing Research, 58,* 853–864; Stanovich, K. E. (1986). Matthew effects in reading: Some consequences of individual differences in the acquisition of literacy. *Reading Research Quarterly, 22,* 360–407.

10. Nagy & Anderson, 1984.

11. Beck, I. L., McKeown, M. G., & Omanson, R. C. (1987). The effects and uses of diverse vocabulary instructional techniques. In M. McKeown & M. Curtis (Eds.), *The nature of vocabulary acquisition* (pp. 147–163). Mahwah, NJ: Erlbaum.

12. Wasik B. A., Hindman A. H., & Snell E. K. (2016). Book reading and vocabulary development: A systematic review. *Early Childhood Research Quarterly, 37,* 39–57.

13. Hayes, D. P., & Ahrens, M. G. (1988). Vocabulary simplifications for children: A special case of "motherese"? *Journal of Child Language, 15,* 395–410.

14. Biemiller, A., & Boote, C. (2006). An effective method for building meaning vocabulary in primary grades. *Journal of Educational Psychology, 98,* 44–62.

15. Lever, R., & Senechal, M. (2011). Discussing stories: On how dialogic reading intervention improves kindergarteners' narrative construction. *Journal of Ex-*

perimental Child Psychology, 108, 1–24; Maynard, K. L., Pullen, P. C., & Coyne, M. D. (2010). Teaching vocabulary to first-grade students through repeated shared storybook reading: A comparison of rich and basic instruction to incidental exposure. *Literacy Research and Instruction, 49,* 209–242.

16. Beck et al., 2013; National Reading Panel. (2000). *Report of the National Reading Panel. Teaching children to read: An evidence-based assessment of the scientific research literature on reading and its implications for reading instruction* (NIH Publication No. 00-4769). Washington, DC: US Government Printing Office.

17. Scott, J. A., & Nagy, W. E. (2009). Developing word consciousness. In M. F. Graves (Ed.), *Essential readings on vocabulary instruction* (pp. 102–112). Newark, DE: International Reading Association.

18. Scott & Nagy, 2009.

19. Graves, M. F. (2000). A vocabulary program to complement and bolster a middle-grade comprehension program. In B. M. Taylor, M. F. Graves, & P. van den Broek (Eds.), *Reading for meaning: Fostering comprehension in the middle grades.* New York, NY: Teachers College Press.

20. Beck et al., 2013.

21. Baker et al., 1998; Beck et al., 1982.

CHAPTER 6

1. Yabroff, J. (2016, September 12). Why Roald Dahl never sugar coated his stories for kids. *Signature.*

2. Cleaver, S., & Richardson, M. (2018). *Read with me: Engaging your young reader in Active Reading.* Lanham, MD: Rowman & Littlefield.

3. van den Broek, P., Beker, K., & Oudega, M. (2015). Inference generation in text comprehension: Automatic and strategic processes in the construction of mental representation. In E. J. O'Brien, A. E. Cook, & R. F. J. Lorch (Eds.), *Inferences during reading* (pp. 94–121). Cambridge, UK: Cambridge University Press.

4. Thurlow, R., & van den Broek, P. (1997). Automaticity and inference generation during reading comprehension. *Reading and Writing Quarterly, 13,* 165–181.

5. Perfetti, C. A., & Stafura, J. Z. (2015). Comprehending implicit meanings in text without making inferences. In E. J. O'Brien, A. E. Cook, & R. F. Lorch (Eds.), *Inferences during reading.* Cambridge, UK: Cambridge University Press.

6. McKoon, G., & Ratcliff, R. (2017). Adults with poor reading skills and the inferences they make during reading. *Scientific Studies of Reading, 21,* 292–305.

7. Richards, J. C., & Anderson, N. A. (2003). How do you know? A strategy to help emergent readers make inferences. *The Reading Teacher, 57,* 290–293.

8. Richards & Anderson, 2003.

9. Richards & Anderson, 2003.

10. Walker, C. M., Gopnik, A., & Ganea, P. A. (2015). Learning to learn from stories: Children's developing sensitivity to the causal structure of fictional worlds. *Child Development, 86,* 310–318.

11. Cleaver & Richardson, 2018.

12. Konrath, S. H., O'Brien, E. H., & Hsing, C. (2010). Changes in dispositional empathy in American college students over time: A meta-analysis. *Personality and Social Psychology Review, 15*(2), 180–198.

13. Wolf, M. (2018). *Reader, Come Home.* New York, NY: HarperCollins.

CHAPTER 7

1. Goodwin, B., & Miller, K. (2012, December/2013, January). Research says: Nonfiction reading promotes student success. *Educational Leadership, 70*(4), 80–82.

2. Yopp, R., & Yopp, H. (2006). Informational texts as read-alouds at school and home. *Journal of Literacy Research, 38,* 37–51.

3. Duke, N. K. (2000). 3.6 minutes per day: The scarcity of informational texts in first grade. *Reading Research Quarterly, 35*(2), 202–224.

4. Heard, G., & McDonough, J. (2009). *A place for wonder: Reading and writing nonfiction in the primary grades.* Portland, ME: Stenhouse.

5. Marzano, R. J. (2000). *A new era of school reform: Going where the research takes us.* Aurora, CO: McREL.

6. Kuhn, K. E., Rausch, C. M., McCarty, T. S., Montgomery, S. E., & Rule, A. C. (2017). Utilizing nonfiction texts to enhance reading comprehension and vocabulary in primary grades. *Early Childhood Education, 45,* 285–296.

7. Hernandez, D. J. (2011). *Double jeopardy: How third grade reading skills and poverty influence high school graduation.* Baltimore, MD: Annie E. Casey Foundation.

8. Robb, L. (2018). The myth of learn to read/read to learn. *Scholastic Instructor Magazine.*

9. Caswell, L. J., & Duke, N. K. (1998). Non-narrative as a catalyst for literacy development. *Language Arts, 75,* 108–117.

10. Meyer, B. J. F., Brandt, D. M., & Bluth, G. J. (1980). Use of top-level structure in text key for reading comprehension of 9th grade students. *Reading Research Quarterly, 16*(1), 72–103.

11. Lorch, R. F., & Lorch, E. P. (1996a). Effects of headings on text recall and summarization. *Contemporary Educational Psychology, 21*(3), 261–278; Lorch, R. F., & Lorch, E. P. (1996b). Effects of organizational signals on the free recall of expository text. *Journal of Educational Psychology, 88*(1), 38–48.

12. Neuman, S. B., Kaefer, T., & Pinkham, A. (2014). Building background knowledge. *The Reading Teacher, 68,* 145–148.

13. Neuman et al., 2014.

14. Kintsch, W. (1988). The role of knowledge in discourse comprehension: A construction-integration model. *Psychological Review,* 95(2), 163–182; Cain, K., Oakhill, J. V., Barnes, M. A., & Bryant, P. E. (2001). Comprehension skill, inference-making ability, and their relation to knowledge. *Memory and Cognition, 29*(6), 850–859.

15. Kintsch, 1988; Cain et al., 2001.

16. Garner, R., Gillingham, M., & White, C. (1989). Effects of "seductive details" on macroprocessing and microprocessing in adults and children. *Cognition and Instruction, 6*(1), 41–57.

17. Armbruster, B. B. (2004). Considerate texts. In D. Lapp, J. Flood, & N. Farnan (Eds.), *Content area reading and learning: Instructional strategies* (2nd ed., pp. 47–58). Mahwah, NJ: Erlbaum.

18. Pyle, N., Vasquez, A. C., Lignugaris, B., Gillam, S. C., & Reutzel, D. R. (2017). Effects of expository text structure interventions on comprehension: A meta-analysis. *Reading Research Quarterly, 52,* 469–501.

19. Fletcher, J. M. (2006). Measuring reading comprehension. *Scientific Studies of Reading, 10*(3), 323–330; Hall, K. M., Sabey, B. L., & McClellan, M. (2005). Expository text comprehension: Helping primary-grade teachers use expository texts to full advantage. *Reading Psychology, 26*(3), 211–234; Kendeou, P., & van den Broek, P. (2007). The effects of prior knowledge and text structure on comprehension processes during reading of scientific texts. *Memory and Cognition, 7*(35), 1567–1577.

20. Maloch, B., & Horsey, M. (2013). Living inquiry: Learning from and about informational texts in a second-grade classroom. *The Reading Teacher, 66,* 475–485.

21. Bortnem, G. M. (2011). Teacher use of interactive read alouds using nonfiction in early childhood classrooms. *Journal of College Teaching and Learning, 5*(12), 29–43.

CHAPTER 8

1. Pope, D. (2012). The early push towards chapter books is a mistake. *New York Times*. Retrieved from https://www.nytimes.com/roomfordebate/2012/12/26/what-books-are-just-right-for-the-young-reader/the-early-push-toward-chapter-books-is-a-mistake

CHAPTER 9

1. The Tennison family names are pseudonyms.

2. Drummond, K. (2019). About reading disabilities, learning disabilities, and reading difficulties. *Reading Rockets.* Retrieved from http://www.readingrockets.org/article/about-reading-disabilities-learning-disabilities-and-reading-difficulties

3. Hoover, W. A., & Gough, P. B. (1999). The simple view of reading. *Reading and Writing: An Interdisciplinary Journal, 2,* 127–160.

4. Engelmann, S. (1986). *Teach your child to read in 100 easy lessons.* New York, NY: Touchstone.

5. Hasbrouck, J., & Tindal, G. (2017). Fluency norms chart (2017 update). *Reading Rockets.* Retrieved from www.readingrockets.org/article/fluency-norms -chart-2017-update

6. Hoover & Gough, 1999.

7. Barnes, M. A., Ahmed, Y., Barth, A., & Francis, D. J. (2015). The relation of knowledge-text integration processes and reading comprehension in 7th- to 12th-grade students. *Scientific Studies of Reading, 19*(4), 253–272; Bowyer-Crane, C., & Snowling, M. J. (2005). Assessing children's inference generation: What do tests of reading comprehension measure? *The British Journal of Educational Psychology, 75*(Pt. 2), 189–201; Cain, K., & Oakhill, J. V. (1999). Inference making ability and its relation to comprehension failure in young children. *Reading and Writing, 11,* 489–503; Cain, K., Oakhill, J. V., Barnes, M. A., & Bryant, P. E. (2001). Comprehension skill, inference-making ability, and their relation to knowledge. *Memory and Cognition, 29,* 850–859.

8. Diakidoy, P., Stylianou, P., Karefillidou, C., Papageorgiou, P. (2005). The relationship between listening and reading comprehension of different types of text at increasing grade levels. *Reading Psychology, 26,* 55–80.

9. Marulis, L. M., & Neuman, S. B. (2010). The effects of vocabulary instruction on young children's word learning: A meta-analysis. *Review of Educational Research, 80,* 300–335.

10. Baker, S. K., Santoro, L. E., Chard, D. J., Fien, H., Park, Y., & Otterstedt, J. (2013). An evaluation of an explicit read aloud intervention taught in whole-classroom formats in first grade. *The Elementary School Journal, 113,* 331–358.

11. Hall, K., & Williams, L. (2010). Teachers' reading aloud of Caldecott Award–winning picture books with diverse first grade children in a high poverty school. *Journal of Research in Childhood Education, 24*(4), 298–314.

12. Swanson, E., Wanzek, J., Petscher, Y., Vaughn, S., Heckert, J., Cavanaugh, C., Kraft, G., & Tackett, K. (2011). A synthesis of read-aloud interventions on early reading outcomes among preschool through third graders at risk for reading difficulties. *Journal of Learning Disabilities, 44,* 258–275.

CHAPTER 10

1. Hoover, W. A., & Gough, P. B. (1999). The simple view of reading. *Reading and Writing: An Interdisciplinary Journal, 2,* 127–160.

2. Wilson, D., & Conyers, M. (2017). A skill strong readers share: Metacognition helps readers analyze texts as they read, and it's a skill you can teach. Edutopia.org. Retrieved from https://www.edutopia.org/article/trait-strong-readers-share

3. Mann, S., & Cadman, R. (2014). Does boredom make us more creative? *Creativity Research Journal, 2,* 165–173.

4. Ungar, M. (2012, June 24). Let kids be bored (occasionally): There are many benefits of letting children amuse themselves this summer. *Psychology Today.* Re-

trieved from https://www.psychologytoday.com/us/blog/nurturing-resilience/201206
/let-kids-be-bored-occasionally

APPENDIX B

1. August, D., & Hakuta, K. (Eds.) (1997). *Improving schooling for language-minority children: A research guide.* Washington, DC: National Academy Press.

2. Huennekens, M. E., & Xu, Y. (2016). Using dialogic reading to enhance emergent literacy skills of young dual language learners. *Early Child Development and Care, 186*(2), 324–340; Tong, F., Lara-Alecio, R., Irby, B., Mathes, P., & Kwok, O.(2008). Accelerating early academic oral English development in transitioning bilingual and structured English immersion programs. *American Educational Research Journal, 45*(4), 1011–1044.

References

Adams, M. J. (1990). *Beginning to read: Thinking and learning about print.* Cambridge, MA: MIT Press.

Anderson, J. R., Finchem, J. L., & Douglass, S. (1997). The role of examples and rules in the acquisition of a cognitive skill. *Journal of Experimental Psychology: Learning, Memory and Cognition, 23,* 932–945.

Anderson, R. C. (1984). Role of reader's schema in comprehension, learning, and memory. In R. C. Anderson, J. Osborn, & R. Tierney (Eds.), *Learning to read in American schools: Basal readers and content texts* (pp. 243–257). Hillsdale, NJ: Lawrence Erlbaum.

Anderson, R. C., Hiebert, E. H., Scott, J. A., & Wilkinson, I. A. S. (1985). *Becoming a nation of readers: The report of the Commission on Reading.* National Institute of Education. Washington, DC: Department of Education.

Anderson, R. C., Nguyen-Jahiel, K., McNurlen, B., Archodidou, A., Kim, S., Reznitskaya, A., et al. (2001). The snowball phenomenon: Spread of ways of talking and ways of thinking across groups of children. *Cognition and Instruction, 19,* 1–46.

Armbruster, B. B. (2004). Considerate texts. In D. Lapp, J. Flood, & N. Farnan (Eds.), *Content area reading and learning: Instructional strategies* (2nd ed., 47–58). Mahwah, NJ: Erlbaum.

August, D., & Hakuta, K. (Eds.) (1997). *Improving schooling for language-minority children: A research guide.* Washington, DC: National Academy Press.

Baker, L., & Stein, N. (1981). The development of prose comprehension skills. In C. Santa & B. Hayes (Eds.), *Children's prose comprehension: Research and practice* (pp. 7–43). Newark, DE: International Reading Association.

Baker, S. K., Santoro, L. E., Chard, D. J., Fien, H., Park, Y., & Otterstedt, J. (2013). An evaluation of an explicit read aloud intervention taught in whole-classroom formats in first grade. *The Elementary School Journal, 113,* 331–358.

Baker, S., Simmons, D., & Kame'enui, E. (1998). *Vocabulary acquisition: Synthesis of the research.* Washington, DC: US Department of Education, Office of Educational Research and Improvement, Educational Resources Information Center.

Barnes, M. A., Ahmed, Y., Barth, A., & Francis, D. J. (2015). The relation of knowledge-text integration processes and reading comprehension in 7th- to 12th-grade students. *Scientific Studies of Reading, 19*(4), 253–272. doi:10.1080/10888438.2015.1022650

Baumann, J. F., & Bergeron, B. S. (1993). Story map instruction using children's literature: Effects on first graders' comprehension of central narrative elements. *Journal of Reading Behavior, 25,* 407–437.

Beck, I. L., McKeown, M. G., & Kucan, L. (2013). *Bringing words to life* (2nd ed.). New York, NY: Guilford.

Beck, I. L., McKeown, M. G., & Omanson, R. C. (1987). The effects and uses of diverse vocabulary instructional techniques. In M. McKeown & M Curtis (Eds.), *The nature of vocabulary acquisition* (pp. 147–163). Mahwah, NJ: Erlbaum.

Beck, I. L., Perfetti, C. A., & McKeown, M. G. (1982). The effects of long-term vocabulary instruction on lexical access and reading comprehension. *Journal of Educational Psychology, 74,* 506–521.

Biemiller, A., & Boote, C. (2006). An effective method for building meaning vocabulary in primary grades. *Journal of Educational Psychology, 98,* 44–62.

Bortnem, G. M. (2011). Teacher use of interactive read alouds using nonfiction in early childhood classrooms. *Journal of College Teaching and Learning, 5*(12), 29–43.

Bowey, J. A. (1986). Syntactic awareness in relation to reading skills and on-going reading comprehension monitoring. *Journal of Experimental Child Psychology, 41,* 282–299.

Bowyer-Crane, C., & Snowling, M. J. (2005). Assessing children's inference generation: What do tests of reading comprehension measure? *The British Journal of Educational Psychology, 75*(Pt. 2), 189–201.

Brabham, E. G., & Lynch-Brown, C. (2002). Effects of teachers' reading-aloud styles on vocabulary acquisition and comprehension of students in the early elementary grades. *Journal of Educational Psychology, 94,* 465–473.

Bransford, J. D., & Johnson, M. K. (1972). Contextual prerequisites for understanding: Some investigations of comprehension and recall. *Journal of Verbal Learning and Verbal Behavior, 11,* 717–726.

Cain, K., Catts, H., Hogan, T., & Loma, R., Language and Reading Research Consortium. (2015). Learning to read: Should we keep things simple? *Reading Research Quarterly, 50,* 151–169.

Cain, K., & Oakhill, J. V. (1999). Inference making ability and its relation to comprehension failure in young children. *Reading and Writing, 11,* 489–503.

Cain, K., & Oakhill, J. (2006a). Matthew effects in young readers: Reading comprehension and reading experience aid vocabulary development. *Journal of Learning Disabilities, 44,* 431–443.

Cain, K., & Oakhill, J. (2006b). Profiles of children with specific reading comprehension difficulties. *British Journal of Educational Psychology, 76*(4), 683–696.

Cain, K., Oakhill, J. V., Barnes, M. A., & Bryant, P. E. (2001). Comprehension skill, inference-making ability, and their relation to knowledge. *Memory and Cognition, 29*(6), 850–859.

Cain, K., Oakhill, J., & Lemmon, K. (2004). Individual differences in the inference of word meanings from context: The influence of reading comprehension, vocabulary knowledge, and memory capacity. *Journal of Educational Psychology, 964,* 671–681.

Calfee, R. C., & Patrick, C. L. (1995). *Teach our children well: Bringing K–12 education into the 21st century.* Stanford, CA: Stanford Alumni.

Caswell, L. J., & Duke, N. K. (1998). Non-narrative as a catalyst for literacy development. *Language Arts, 75,* 108–117.

Catts, H. W. (2018). The simple view of reading: Advancements and false impressions. *Remedial and Special Education, 39,* 317–323.

Catts, H. W., Fey, M. E., Zhang, X., & Tomblin, J. B. (1999). Language basis of reading and reading disabilities: Evidence from a longitudinal investigation. *Scientific Studies of Reading, 3,* 331–361.

Catts, H. W., Hogan, T., & Adlof, S. (2005). Developmental changes in reading and reading disabilities. In H. Catts & A. Kamhi (Eds.), *Connections between language and reading disabilities* (pp. 25–40). Mahwah, NJ: Lawrence Erlbaum; Language and Reading Research Consortium.

Cleaver, S., & Richardson, M. (2018). *Read with me: Engaging your young reader in Active Reading.* Lanham, MD: Rowman & Littlefield.

Connor, C. M., Spencer, M., Day, S. L., Giuliani, S., Ingebrand, S. W., Mclean, L., & Morrison, F. J. (2014). Capturing the complexity: Content, type, and amount of instruction and quality of the classroom learning environment synergistically predict third graders' vocabulary and reading comprehension outcomes. *Journal of Educational Psychology, 106,* 762–778.

Cunningham, A. E., & Stanovich, K. E. (1997). Early reading acquisition and its relation to reading experience and ability 10 years later. *Developmental Psychology, 33,* 934–945.

de Jong, P. F., & Leseman, P. P. M. (2001). Lasting effects of home literacy on reading achievement at school. *Journal of School Psychology, 39*(5), 389–414.

de Jong, P. F., & van der Leij, A. (2002). Effects of phonological abilities and linguistic comprehension on the development of reading. *Scientific Studies of Reading, 6,* 51–77.

Diakidoy, P., Stylianou, P., Karefillidou, C., & Papageorgiou, P. (2005). The relationship between listening and reading comprehension of different types of text and increasing grade levels. *Reading Psychology, 26,* 55–80.

Dickinson, D. K., & Smith, M. W. (1994). Long-term effects of preschool teachers' book readings on low-income children's vocabulary and story comprehension. *Reading Research Quarterly, 29,* 104–122.

Drummond, K. (2019). About reading disabilities, learning disabilities, and reading difficulty. *Reading Rockets.* Retrieved from http://www.readingrockets.org/article/about-reading-disabilities-learning-disabilities-and-reading-difficulties

Duff, D., Tomblin, J. B., & Catts, H. (2015). The influence of reading on vocabulary growth: A case for a Matthew effect. *Journal of Speech, Language, and Hearing Research, 58,* 853–864.

Duke, N. K. (2000). 3.6 minutes per day: The scarcity of informational texts in first grade. *Reading Research Quarterly, 35*(2), 202–224.

Dymock, S. (2007). Comprehension strategy instruction: Teaching narrative text structure awareness. *The Reading Teacher, 61*(2).

Egalite, A. J. (2016). How family background influences student achievement. *Education Next, 16*(2). Retrieved from https://www.educationnext.org/how-family -background-influences-student-achievement/

Engelmann, S. (1986). *Teach your child to read in 100 easy lessons.* New York, NY: Touchstone.

Epstein, B. J. (2017, February 6). Why children's books that teach diversity are more important than ever. *The Conversation.* Retrieved from https://theconversation .com/why-childrens-books-that-teach-diversity-are-more-important-than-ever -72146

Evans, M. D. R., Kelley, J., & Sikora, J. (2014). Scholarly culture and academic performance in 42 nations. *Social Forces, 92,* 1573–1605.

Fisher, D., & Frey, N. (2016, February 15). Questioning that deepens comprehension. *Edutopia.* Retrieved from www.edutopia.org/blog/questioning-that-deepens -comprehension-douglas-fisher-nancy-frey.

Fleming, J., Capatano, S., Thompson, C. M., & Carrillo, S. R. (2016). *More mirrors in the classroom: Using urban children's literature to increase literacy.* Lanham, MD: Rowman & Littlefield.

Fletcher, J. M. (2006). Measuring reading comprehension. *Scientific Studies of Reading, 10*(3), 323–330.

Garner, R., Gillingham, M., & White, C. (1989) Effects of "seductive details" on macroprocessing and microprocessing in adults and children. *Cognition and Instruction, 6*(1), 41–57.

Goodwin, B., & Miller, K. (2012, December/ 2013, January). Research says: Nonfiction reading promotes student success. *Educational Leadership, 70*(4), 80–82.

Graves, M. F. (2000). A vocabulary program to complement and bolster a middle-grade comprehension program. In B. M. Taylor, M. F. Graves, & P. van den Broek (Eds.), *Reading for meaning: Fostering comprehension in the middle grades.* New York, NY: Teachers College Press.

Hall, K. M., Sabey, B. L., & McClellan, M. (2005). Expository text comprehension: Helping primary-grade teachers use expository texts to full advantage. *Reading Psychology, 26*(3), 211–234.

Hall, K., & Williams, L. (2010). Teachers' reading aloud of Caldecott Award–winning picture books with diverse first grade children in a high poverty school. *Journal of Research in Childhood Education, 24*(4), 298–314.

Hasbrouck, J., & Tindal, G. (2017). Fluency norms chart (2017 update). *Reading Rockets.* Retrieved from www.readingrockets.org/article/fluency-norms-chart -2017-update

Hayes, D. P., & Ahrens, M. G. (1988). Vocabulary simplifications for children: A special case of "motherese"? *Journal of Child Language, 15,* 395–410.

Heard, G., & McDonough, J. (2009). *A place for wonder: Reading and writing nonfiction in the primary grades.* Portland, ME: Stenhouse.

Hernandez, D. J. (2011). *Double jeopardy: How third grade reading skills and poverty influence high school graduation.* Baltimore, MD: Annie E. Casey Foundation.

Hogan, T. P., Adlof, S. M., & Alonzo, C. (2014). On the importance of listening comprehension. *Journal of Speech Language Pathology, 16*(3), 199–207.

Hoover, W. A., & Gough, P. B. (1999). The simple view of reading. *Reading and Writing: An Interdisciplinary Journal, 2,* 127–160.

Huennekens, M. E., & Xu, Y. (2016). Using dialogic reading to enhance emergent literacy skills of young dual language learners. Early Child Development and Care, 186(2), 324–340.

Hutton, J., Xu, Y., DeWitt, T., Horowitz-Kraus, T., & Ittenbach, R. (2018, May). Goldilocks effect? Illustrated story format seems "just right" and animation "too hot" for integration of functional brain networks in preschool-aged children. Pediatric Academic Societies, Toronto, Canada. https://www.eurekalert.org/pub_releases/2018-05/pas-nsm042618.php

Huyck, D., & Dahlen, S. P. (2019). Diversity in children's books 2018. *Sarahpark .com* blog. Created in consultation with Edith Campbell, Molly Beth Griffin, K. T. Horning, Debbie Reese, Ebony Elizabeth Thomas, and Madeline Tyner, with statistics compiled by the Cooperative Children's Book Center, School of Education, University of Wisconsin–Madison: ccbc.education.wisc.edu/books/pcstats.asp. Retrieved from readingspark.wordpress.com/2019/06/19/picture-this-diversity-in-childrens-books-2018-infographic

Jackson, S. (2009). The lottery. In *The lottery and other stories.* New York, NY: Penguin. (Original work published in *The New Yorker* magazine on June 26, 1948.)

Kendeou, P., & van den Broek, P. (2007). The effects of prior knowledge and text structure on comprehension processes during reading of scientific texts. *Memory and Cognition, 7*(35), 1567–1577.

Kintsch, W. (1988). The role of knowledge in discourse comprehension: A construction-integration model. *Psychological Review, 95*(2), 163–182.

Klecan-Aker, J. S., & Caraway, T. H. (1997). A study of the relationship of storytelling ability and reading comprehension in fourth and sixth grade: African American children. *European Journal of Disorders of Communication, 32,* 109–125.

Konrath, S. H., O'Brien, E. H., & Hsing, C. (2010). Changes in dispositional empathy in American college students over time: A meta-analysis. *Personality and Social Psychology Review, 15*(2), 180–198.

Kuhn, K. E., Rausch, C. M., McCarty, T. S., Montgomery, S. E., & Rule, A. C. (2017). Utilizing nonfiction texts to enhance reading comprehension and vocabulary in primary grades. *Early Childhood Education, 45,* 285–296.

Lever, R., & Senechal, M. (2011). Discussing stories: On how dialogic reading intervention improves kindergarteners' narrative construction. *Journal of Experimental Child Psychology, 108,* 1–24.

Liu, Y., Liu, H., & Hau, K. (2016). Reading ability development from kindergarten to junior secondary: Latent transition analyses with growth mixture modeling. *Frontier Psychology, 7*.

Lonigan, C. J., & Whitehurst, G. J. (1998). Relative efficacy of parent and teacher involvement in a shared-reading intervention for preschool children from low-income backgrounds. *Early Childhood Research Quarterly, 13*(2), 263–290.

Lorch, R. F., & Lorch, E. P. (1996a). Effects of headings on text recall and summarization. *Contemporary Educational Psychology, 21*(3), 261–278.

Lorch, R. F., & Lorch, E. P. (1996b). Effects of organizational signals on the free recall of expository text. *Journal of Educational Psychology, 88*(1), 38–48.

Mackenzie, S. (2018). *The read-aloud family: Making meaningful and lasting connections with your kids.* Grand Rapids, MI: Zondervan.

Maloch, B., & Horsey, M. (2013). Living inquiry: Learning from and about informational texts in a second-grade classroom. *The Reading Teacher, 66,* 475–485.

Mann, S., & Cadman, R. (2014). Does boredom make us more creative? *Creativity Research Journal, 2,* 165–173.

Marulis, L. M., & Neuman, S. B. (2010). The effects of vocabulary intervention on young children's word learning: A meta-analysis. *Review of Educational Research, 80,* 300–335.

Marzano, R. J. (2000). *A new era of school reform: Going where the research takes us.* Aurora, CO: McREL.

Maynard, K. L., Pullen, P. C., & Coyne, M. D. (2010). Teaching vocabulary to first-grade students through repeated shared storybook reading: A comparison of rich and basic instruction to incidental exposure. *Literacy Research and Instruction, 49,* 209–242.

McKoon, G., & Ratcliff, R. (2017). Adults with poor reading skills and the inferences they make during reading. *Scientific Studies of Reading, 21,* 292–305.

Meyer, B. J. F., Brandt, D. M., & Bluth, G. J. (1980). Use of top-level structure in text key for reading comprehension of 9th grade students. *Reading Research Quarterly, 16*(1), 72–103.

Mol, S. E., Bus, A. G., & de Jong, M. T. (2009). Interactive book reading in early education: A tool to stimulate print knowledge as well as oral language. *Review of Educational Research, 79,* 979–1007.

Nagy, W., & Anderson, R. C. (1984). How many words are there in printed school English? *Reading Research Quarterly, 19,* 304–330.

Nagy W., Herman P., & Anderson R. C. (1985). Learning words from context. *Reading Research Quarterly, 20,* 233–253.

Nation, K., & Snowling, M. J. (1998). Semantic processing and the development of word-recognition skills: Evidence from children with reading comprehension difficulties. *Journal of Memory and Language, 39,* 85–101.

National Reading Panel. (2000). *Report of the National Reading Panel. Teaching children to read: An evidence-based assessment of the scientific research literature on reading and its implications for reading instruction* (NIH Publication No. 00-4769). Washington, DC: US Government Printing Office.

Nelson-Herber, J., & Johnston, C. S. (1989). Questions and concerns about teaching narrative and expository text. In K. D. Muth (Ed.), *Children's comprehension of text: Research into practice* (pp. 263–280). Newark, DE: International Reading Association.

Neuman, S. B., Kaefer, T., & Pinkham, A. (2014). Building background knowledge. *The Reading Teacher, 68,* 145–148.

Nir, S. M. (2018, November 5). Mystery in a small town: Couple shot dead, their daughter missing. *New York Times.* Retrieved from www.nytimes.com/2018/11/05/us/jayme-closs-missing-girl-barron-wisconsin.html

Nye, C., Turner, H., & Schwartz, J. (2006). *Approaches to parent involvement for improving the academic performance of elementary school age children.* Oslo, Norway: Campbell Collaboration.

Oakhill, J. V., & Cain, K. (2012). The precursors of reading ability in young readers: Evidence from a four-year longitudinal study. *Scientific Studies of Reading, 16*(2), 91–121.

Pearson, D. P., Valencia, S. W., & Wixson, K. (2014). Complicating the world of reading assessment: Toward better assessments for better teaching. *Theory into Practice, 53,* 236–246.

Perfetti, C. A., & Stafura, J. Z. (2015). Comprehending implicit meanings in text without making inferences. In E. J. O'Brien, A. E. Cook, & R. F. Lorch (Eds.), *Inferences during reading.* Cambridge, UK: Cambridge University Press.

Pope, D. (2012). The early push towards chapter books is a mistake. *New York Times.* Retrieved from https://www.nytimes.com/roomfordebate/2012/12/26/what-books-are-just-right-for-the-young-reader/the-early-push-toward-chapter-books-is-a-mistake

Pyle, N., Vasquez, A. C., Lignugaris, B., Gillam, S. C., & Reutzel, D. R. (2017). Effects of expository text structure interventions on comprehension: A meta-analysis. *Reading Research Quarterly, 52,* 469–501.

Reznitskaya, A., Anderson, R. C., McNurlen, B., Nguyen-Jahiel, K., Archodidou, A., & Kim, S. (2001). Influence of oral discussion on written argument. *Discourse Processes, 32,* 155–175.

Richards, J. C., & Anderson, N. A. (2003). How do you know? A strategy to help emergent readers make inferences. *The Reading Teacher, 57,* 290–293.

Robb, L. (2018). The myth of learn to read/read to learn. *Scholastic Instructor Magazine.*

Roth, F. P., Speece, D. L., & Cooper, D. H. (2002). A longitudinal analysis of the connection between oral language and early reading. *The Journal of Education Research, 95*(5), 259–272.

Scholastic. (2016). *Kids and family reading report.* Retrieved from https://www.scholastic.com/readingreport/home.html

Scott, J. A., & Nagy, W. E. (2009). Developing word consciousness. In M. F. Graves (Ed.), *Essential readings on vocabulary instruction* (pp. 102–112). Newark, DE: International Reading Association.

Smolkin, L. B., & Donovan, C. A. (2001).The contexts of comprehension: The information book read-aloud, comprehension acquisition, and comprehension instruction in a first-grade classroom. *Elementary School Journal, 102,* 97–122.

Snow, C. E., Burns, S., & Griffin, P. (Eds.). (1998). *Preventing reading difficulties in young children.* Washington, DC: National Academies Press.

Stanovich, K. E. (1986). Matthew effects in reading: Some consequences of individual differences in the acquisition of literacy. *Reading Research Quarterly, 22,* 360–407.

Storch, S. A., & Whitehurst, G. J. (2002). Oral language and code-related precursors to reading: Evidence from a longitudinal structural model. *Developmental Psychology, 38,* 934–947.

Swaburn, M. S. L., & de Glopper, K. (1999). Incidental word learning while reading: A meta-analysis. *Review of Educational Research, 69,* 261–285.

Swanson, E., Wanzek, J., Petscher, Y., Vaughn, S., Heckert, J., Cavanaugh, C., Kraft, G., & Tackett, K. (2011). A synthesis of read-aloud interventions on early reading outcomes among preschool through third graders at risk for reading difficulties. *Journal of Learning Disabilities, 44,* 258–275.

Tamer, M. T., & Walsh, B. (2016). *Raising strong readers: Strategies for parents and educators to encourage children to read from infancy to high school.* Retrieved from https://www.gse.harvard.edu/news/uk/16/03/raising-strong-readers

Tankersly, K. (2003). *The threads of reading.* Alexandria, VA: ASCD.

Thurlow, R., & van den Broek, P. (1997). Automaticity and inference generation during reading comprehension. *Reading and Writing Quarterly, 13,* 165–181.

Tilstra, J., McMaster, K., van den Broek, P., Kendeou, P., & Rapp, D. (2009). Simple but complex: Components of the simple view of reading across grade levels. *Journal of Research in Reading, 32,* 383–401.

Tong, F., Lara-Alecio, R., Irby, B., Mathes, P., & Kwok, O. (2008). Accelerating early academic oral English development in transitioning bilingual and structured *English immersion programs. American Educational Research Journal, 45*(4), 1011–1044.

Torgesen, J., & Davis, C. (1996). Individual difference variables that predict response to training in phonological awareness. *Journal of Experimental Child Psychology, 63,* 1–21.

Trabasso, T. (1981). Can we integrate research and instruction on reading comprehension? In C. Santa & B. Hayes (Eds.), *Children's prose comprehension: Research and practice* (pp. 103–116). Newark, DE: International Reading Association.

Trabasso, T., & Wiley, J. (2005). Goal plans of action and inferences during comprehension of narratives. *Discourse Processes, 39,* 129–164.

Trelease, J. (2013). *The read-aloud handbook* (7th ed.). New York, NY: Penguin.

Ungar, M. (2012, June 24). Let kids be bored (occasionally): There are many benefits of letting children amuse themselves this summer. *Psychology Today.* Retrieved from https://www.psychologytoday.com/us/blog/nurturing-resilience/201206/let-kids-be-bored-occasionally

van den Broek, P., Beker, K., & Oudega, M. (2015). Inference generation in text comprehension: Automatic and strategic processes in the construction of mental representation. In E. J. O'Brien, A. E. Cook, & R. F. J. Lorch (Eds.), *Inferences during reading* (pp. 94–121). Cambridge, UK: Cambridge University Press.

van den Broek, P., Kendeou, P., Kremer, K., Lynch, J., Butler, J., White, M. J., et al. (2005). Assessment of comprehension abilities in young children. In S. G. Paris & S. A. Stahl (Eds.), *Children's reading comprehension and assessment* (pp. 107–130). Mahwah, NJ: Lawrence Erlbaum.

Verhoeven, L., van Leeuwe, J., & Vermeer, A. (2011). Vocabulary growth and reading development across the elementary school years. *Scientific Studies of Reading, 15,* 8–25.

Walker, C. M., Gopnik, A., & Ganea, P. A. (2015). Learning to learn from stories: Children's developing sensitivity to the causal structure of fictional worlds. *Child Development, 86,* 310–318.

Warren, C., Edwards, D., Isenberg, S., & Oldani, J. (2010). Effects of at-home reading activities and parental involvement on classroom reading scores: Focus on the elementary years. ProQuest Dissertations.

Wasik, B. A., & Bond, M. A. (2001). Beyond the pages of a book: Interactive book reading and language development in pre-school classrooms. *Journal of Educational Psychology, 93*(2), 243–250.

Wasik B. A., Hindman A. H., & Snell E. K. (2016). Book reading and vocabulary development: A systematic review. *Early Childhood Research Quarterly, 37,* 39–57.

Wegerif, R., Mercer, N., & Dawes, L. (1999). From social interaction to individual reasoning: An empirical investigation of a possible sociocultural model of cognitive development. *Learning and Instruction, 9,* 493–516.

Whitehurst, G. J., Arnold, D. S., Epstein, J. N., Angell, A. L., Smith, M., & Fischel, J. E. (1994). A picture book reading intervention in day care and home for children from low-income families. *Developmental Psychology, 30*(5), 679–689.

Wilson, D., & Conyers, M. (2017). A skill strong readers share: Metacognition helps readers analyze texts as they read, and it's a skill you can teach your students. https://www.edutopia.org/article/trait-strong-readers-share

Wise, J. C., Sevcik, R. A., Morris, R. D., Lovett, M. W., & Wolf, M. (2007). The relationship among receptive and expressive vocabulary, listening comprehension, pre-reading skills, word identification skills, and reading comprehension by children with reading disabilities. *Journal of Speech, Language, and Hearing Research, 50,* 1093–1109.

Wolf, M. (2018). *Reader, come home.* New York, NY: HarperCollins.

Yabroff, J. (2016, September 12). Why Roald Dahl never sugar coated his stories for kids. *Signature.* Retrieved from http://www.signature-reads.com/2016/09/why-roald-dahl-never-sugar-coated-his-stories-for-kids/

Yopp, R., & Yopp, H. (2006). Informational texts as read-alouds at school and home. *Journal of Literacy Research, 38,* 37–51.

Zwiers, J., & Crawford, M. (2011). *Academic conversations: Classroom talk that fosters critical thinking and content understanding.* Portsmouth, NH: Stenhouse.

About the Author

Samantha Cleaver grew up in Chicago, Illinois. She taught special education and worked as an instructional coach before moving to Charlotte, North Carolina, where she helped lead the initial design and startup of Active Reading work for Read Charlotte, a community-wide initiative to double the number of students reading on grade level by third grade in Mecklenburg County. She earned a doctorate in special education with a focus on literacy interventions from the University of North Carolina at Charlotte. Currently, she works at a local middle school teaching English language arts and math. She has three young children who are growing into Active Readers. Her favorite books to read with her children are *Where the Wild Things Are by* Maurice Sendak, *Strictly No Elephants* by Lisa Mantchev, and the *Finn Family Moomintroll* books by Tove Jansson.